WARNING: This book is not for heroes or saints or perfectionists.

This book is for flawed people (and we are all flawed in one way or another) who are not happy with the way things are and would like to make a difference.

This book is for ordinary people who want to make connections that create extraordinary outcomes.

GETTING TO MAYBE HOW

Frances Westley

Brenda Zimmerman

and Michael Quinn Patton

THE WORLD IS CHANGED

Random House Canada

www.randomhouse.ca

LIBRARY AND ARCHIVES CANADA CATALOGUING IN PUBLICATION

Westley, Frances
      Getting to maybe : how the world is changed / Frances Westley, Brenda Zimmerman & Michael Quinn Patton.

ISBN-13: 978-0-679-31443-1
ISBN-10: 0-679-31443-1

      1. Social action. I. Patton, Michael Quinn
II. Zimmerman, Brenda, 1956– III. Title.
HN18.3.W48 2006   361.2'5   C2006-903008-1

Jacket and text design: CS Richardson

Printed and bound in the United States of America

10 9 8 7 6 5 4 3 2 1

Contents

Foreword

Assume hope, all you who enter here.

When he was still in prison, serving a sentence of four and half years' hard labour for his human rights activities in defiance of the communist regime, long before he became president of Czechoslovakia—and long before, I suppose, there was even the remotest notion in his mind that he would be president or indeed that democracy would be restored any time soon in his beloved country—Valclav Havel wrote this about hope in a letter to his wife, Olga: "Hope is a dimension of the spirit. It is not outside us, but within us." Many months later he wrote: "The more I think about it, the more I incline to the opinion that the most important thing of all is not to lose hope and faith in life itself . . . This doesn't mean closing one's eyes to the horrors of the world—quite the contrary, in fact." Havel made a critical distinction between hope and optimism: "[Hope] is not the conviction that something will turn out well, but the certainty that something makes sense, regardless of how it turns out."

Havel's story and his wisdom are lessons for all of us who have a desire for transformative effect in a world that so often seems so unyielding.

Here's another: in the mid-fifteenth century, for several decades prior to the European discovery of America, people were certain that the end was nigh. There was a kind of apocalypse watch in effect. The authoritative *Nuremberg Chronicle* provided blank pages for readers to record signs and portents of the impending end.

Of course, the end was not nigh. Nor were the riches of India. But when Columbus sailed out on the curved sea, everything changed. An unimaginable future began to take shape.

If history shows us anything, it's that the obdurate world *does* yield. Change—surprising and sometimes radical change—*does* happen. The world does turn on its head every once in a while. And what seemed almost impossible looking forward seems almost inevitable looking back.

—

We are living at a point in history when the need and desire for change is profound. Our current trajectory is no longer sustainable. We cannot ignore the compelling environmental and social challenges that vex today's world because they will undermine us all. We cannot dismiss the fractures in our own communities, or the fissures between those of us fortunate to live in comfort and the massive number of our fellow human beings who live under the crush of poverty around the world.

It is a pivotal time. We need to be change-makers—and very capable ones at that. Over the past two hundred years, human society has developed exceptional ingenuities, proficiencies, organizations and systems for the task of making *things*—from steam engines to microchips. Going forward, we must learn to be equally adept at the task of making *change*. It's an essential modern competency. In fact, the challenge of change has begun to draw an interesting and diverse assortment of players, and their numbers have been growing over the last few years. I have been in the business of social change for more than twenty-five years. The recent growth in the field has been astonishing to observe. It is evidence of the urgency of the challenges we face and an indication that social change has moved from the margins to the mainstream. But how can we move the dial on our most complex and seemingly intractable social problems? How can we be more than just anxious critics of the status quo or wishful thinkers about a better future, and become actual and effective agents for large-scale transformations?

These are the questions that *Getting to Maybe* sets out to address. There are no simple formulas—serious and significant social change necessarily involves recognizing and dealing with complex systems, which seem to operate with a logic and life of their own, are far from inert, and battle (like the living organisms with which we are more familiar) for their own preservation. But if you're willing to open your mind to the *nature* of these systems, you will discover a world of possibility.

This book is about the art, the science and the experience of possibility. Its bold purpose is to change the way we change the world. Again and again, you'll see from the examples it contains that change seems to be a process that can be tapped but not muscled. The science of complexity, admirably brought to life in the pages that follow, helps us to see the world through a different lens, to make a fundamental shift in perception—from complexity as obstacle to complexity as opportunity.

—

I have been asked by the authors to say something about the genesis of this book. The story goes back to the fall of 1999, when I was approached by a senior executive at DuPont Canada to help them with the development of their corporate citizenship strategy. He told me they were not interested in just making charitable contributions to worthy causes—they wanted to find a way to make a significant difference. As I began my investigations and came to learn more about DuPont, I was struck by the fact that this is one of the world's great innovation-driven companies. The culture of innovation is powerful inside DuPont and has been central to the company's success throughout its long history. As DuPont says, "We didn't get where we wanted to go by taking baby steps. We got there by taking leaps . . . leaps that have changed everything."

Because my own work involves the development of large-scale social change projects, and because I've had the opportunity over the years to tackle a very broad range of social challenges (ranging from AIDS prevention to environmental protection, from civic engagement to using sport and play to improve the lives of the world's most disadvantaged children) with a broad range of clients (in the public, private and voluntary sectors), I had become increasingly convinced of the need for radical innovation linked to a systems approach amongst those who are working to make a difference.

So I made a pretty bold recommendation to DuPont. I suggested that they make *social innovation itself* their cause of choice: help foster the development of new mindsets and new skill-sets for achieving large-scale pattern-shifting impact. Draw on the company's own invaluable knowledge assets—developed over many years by being deliberate, thoughtful and scientific about complex systems and the human, organizational and collaborative processes necessary to achieve innovation. These "processes," as DuPont put it, "get partners working together to a higher-order purpose on complex challenges to achieve breakthrough results."

I fully expected to be shot down. This suggestion was about as far out on a limb as any corporate citizenship program I was aware of. It was difficult to envision, more difficult still to communicate. It would take a long time and a lot of hard work before there were any payoffs. It had no simple hooks to give it ready emotional resonance for the public.

But DuPont has a big appetite for bold, problem-solving challenges. They not only got the concept, they leapt at it. Ron Zelonka, who was the executive vice-president in charge of the Research and Business Development Unit, as well as a brilliant scientist, created the Social Innovation Enterprise under his wing, and hired two staff members from within DuPont—Colleen Brydon and Chris DeGrow—to run it. (A few years later, Lori Sommers would take the helm.)

As a first step, I convened a round table of about a dozen leaders from Canada's social sector to meet with the DuPont team and explore the opportunity to promote social innovation and refine our initial thinking. One of the participants we invited was Frances Westley, a co-author of this book. Frances had designed and was directing the McGill-McConnell Program for National Voluntary Sector Leaders, an executive MBA for the non-profit sector. It was unique in North America, truly innovative in its approach and highly consequential in its effects. I think it's fair to say that the attendees were impressed by DuPont's commitment to foster social innovation. By the end of the session they recognized the seriousness of the company's intention, the depth of knowledge they could bring to the challenge, and the rare combination of courage and humility with which they were venturing forth.

Once the Social Innovation Enterprise was operational, we formed a working alliance with a community development initiative called Opportunities 2000, whose mission was "to create bold solutions that reduce and prevent poverty" in the Waterloo region of Ontario, about ninety kilometres down the road from DuPont Canada's headquarters (for a full description of the project see pages 145–151). Soon after, DuPont formed another key partnership with the Ontario Science Centre. The science centre was at the formative stages of a dynamic new venture—its leap into the twenty-first century—driven by a goal congruent with that of the Social Innovation Enterprise: to promote a culture of innovation and collaborative problem-solving to help equip a new generation to meet the challenges and opportunities of the future.

In early 2002, Chris, Colleen and I began to consider the best path for the Social Innovation Enterprise. We shared a conviction that the richest opportunity lay upstream, in research and knowledge development: advancing knowledge about social innovation so that it could advance the work of change-makers. We reconnected with Frances Westley to explore the possibility of forming a joint initiative at McGill. From these deliberations, the McGill-Dupont Social Innovation Think Tank was born.

Frances is a master at many things, not the least of which is the design of brilliant cross-cutting collaborative processes. She recruited two eminent academic colleagues, Brenda Zimmerman and Michael Patton, who eventually also became her co-authors. In addition to their own scholarship, they, too, had considerable experience on the social change front, working with voluntary sector and government organizations. Warren Nilsson and Nada Fara, both doctoral candidates at McGill's Faculty of Management, came on board as research associates and active participants. Along with Chris, Colleen and myself, this made up the think-tank team.

We were a hybrid group and we followed a hybrid process. We brought ideas, insights and hunches shaped by our respective individual experiences to the table. We drew on research and theory about transformative processes from a broad cross-section of sciences—from biology and ecology to behavioural psychology and management to network analysis, chaos and complexity theory. We identified a variety of examples of successful social change initiatives and examined them for detectable—and informative—patterns of congruence. We consulted leading social innovators to gain insights about lived experiences. And we engaged some world-leading thinkers, among them Henry Mintzberg, C.S. (Buzz) Holling, William Isaacs and Thomas Homer-Dixon, to participate in our working sessions.

Getting to Maybe was born of those inspiring discussions with some of the leading players in the field. What drove us was not the idea that we could create something definitive, but the hope that it could be generative. That we could constellate some of the diverse knowledge of transformative processes with actual case studies of significant social change. We believed that ways of seeing could change ways of doing, that influencing perspective could influence practice that in turn could influence progress. Coming out of the work of the think-tank, and drawing on their own rich experience as academics and practitioners, Frances, Brenda and Michael have created *Getting to Maybe*.

—

Perhaps *Getting to Maybe* strikes you as an odd title for a book whose core message is a powerful statement of hope and profound possibility. Until you recognize that "maybe" so accurately describes our fundamental relationship to the world. It is a relationship in which time is one of the critical dimensions—a relationship to what is ahead, a relationship that is constantly unfolding.

The world ahead is what calls to us, compels our judgments and commands our actions.

The world commands us. We do not command it. And yet—it yields. So "maybe" becomes a potent word for the brave, the inventive, the adventurous. Maybe, just maybe, we can discover a way to save a species, prevent an epidemic of disease or violence, help lift people out of poverty and indignity, break the grip of intolerance, lighten our footprint on the fragile earth.

"Maybe" comes with no guarantees, only a chance. But "maybe" has always been the best odds the world has offered to those who set out to alter its course—to find a new land across the sea, to end slavery, to enable women to vote, to walk on the moon, to bring down the Berlin Wall.

"Maybe" is not a cautious word. It is a defiant claim of possibility in the face of a status quo we are unwilling to accept. And as you will see from reading this book, transforming the world *is* possible because the very complex forces of interconnection that make systems resistant to change are the same ones that can be harnessed to propel change.

"Maybe" is hope incarnate—for all but the complacent and the cynical.

This book is for the rest of you.

—ERIC YOUNG, PRESIDENT, E.Y.E.

KOEYE, B.C., JUNE 2006

Our deepest fear is not that we are inadequate. Our deepest fear is that we are powerful beyond measure. It is our light, not our darkness that most frightens us. We ask ourselves, who am I to be brilliant, gorgeous, talented fabulous? Actually, who are you *not* to be? . . . Your playing small does not serve the world. There's nothing enlightened about shrinking so that other people won't feel insecure around you. We are all meant to shine, as children do. . . . It is not just in some of us; it is in everyone. And as we let our own light shine, we unconsciously give other people permission to do the same. As we are liberated from our own fear, our presence automatically liberates others.

—Marianne Williamson, *A Return to Love*

Light the first light of evening, as in a room
In which we rest and, for small reason, think
The world imagined is the ultimate good.

Wallace Stevens, "Final Soliloquy
of the Interior Paramour"

1. The First Light of Evening

From 1984 to the autumn of 1985, Bob Geldof, the lead singer of Irish rock band the Boomtown Rats, raised over sixty million pounds for famine relief in Ethiopia.[1] He did it by organizing Band Aid, first cutting a best-selling song in collaboration with British rock stars and then organizing a huge Live Aid telethon, which lasted seventeen hours and was broadcast from both sides of the Atlantic. Geldof was seized with the determination to help the starving of Ethiopia while watching a BBC documentary on the famine. Hundreds of people were involved in making Live Aid successful, but the vision behind the effort was his. Live Aid not only set a standard for international rock concerts, but also tapped a new charitable niche—youth—and challenged the aid delivery system set up by governments and non-governmental organizations (NGOs). Geldof worked out a strategy that allowed him to use the expertise and distribution systems of existing aid organizations while he cut through much of the red tape that traditionally slowed aid delivery.

While Live Aid did not solve the problem of famine in Africa, Geldof was widely praised for his innovative contribution. He has been knighted, won numerous awards, and was nominated in 1986 for the Nobel Peace Prize. And yet, in many ways he was an unlikely hero. By his own admission, he was a marginally successful musician who had been leading a desolate life and making little effort to contribute to anything other than his musical career. He had been born poor and never received much of an education. As one journalist wrote, "God opened the door and saw this scruffy Irishman and said, 'Oh what the heck, he'll do.'"

And he did.

—

In 1997, the World Bank reported that an estimated thirty million people had contracted HIV/AIDS and 90 percent of them were in developing countries.[2] Statistics from the UN show this number had climbed to forty million by 2004 and is predicted to climb by another twenty million in the next two decades. Among those countries hardest hit is South Africa, which has the highest number of infected people of any country.

By any number of measures, Brazil should be at the top of the list with South Africa. In 1990, Brazil had almost twice as many cases of HIV/AIDS as South Africa, and a World Bank study predicted that Brazil would have off-the-chart infection rates for HIV/AIDS by the turn of the millennium. The World Bank researchers told Brazil to focus on prevention—and in effect to be prepared to lose all those infected before the epidemic was under control.[3]

At the start of the new millennium, as predicted, one in four people in South Africa were infected with HIV. However, in Brazil, a miracle occurred: the country's infection rate had dropped to 0.6 percent (1 in 160). Today, Brazil is touted as a model for developing countries fighting HIV/AIDS. How did this miracle happen?

If you look for a charismatic leader who inspired the people, you quickly realize there wasn't one. Instead, Brazilians at all levels, from government bureaucrats to local community leaders, joined forces in the service of a key guiding principle: no person, no matter how poor, insignificant or illiterate, could be written off as beyond cure. Liberation theology, a version of Catholicism that infuses Brazilian culture, proclaims the importance of empowering the poor and creating liberty for all. Health care workers looked for ways to ensure treatment would be available to all citizens regardless of their ability to pay and found resources that were hidden from external observers and HIV/AIDS experts. Volunteers from churches and other non-health charities worked alongside the clinical experts, and became invaluable in both helping people follow complicated drug regimens and learning ways to prevent infection. At the government level, a clause in an international trade agreement was used to wage a successful legal battle for the right to make generic drugs in cases of national emergency, which reduced the price of HIV/AIDS drugs.

To spread the prevention message, the Brazilians decided to use humour rather than fear. Clowns wearing costumes made of condoms handed out condom lollipops to drive home the safe-sex message in a fun and memorable way. One playful billboard depicted three beautiful women sitting around a condom-shaped table. The thought bubbles above their heads all said "Si." The message was that women will say yes, yes, yes to men who use condoms! These campaigns were in stark contrast to those in most other countries, which stressed "Use condoms or you could die." Clearly Brazilians did not want anyone to die of AIDS. But they reasoned that youth, who were the most susceptible to contracting HIV, often feel invulnerable and rarely are thinking about death, especially when they are contemplating sex.

—

Live Aid is a miracle in close-up, which in our awestruck or inadequate moments we can put down to the actions of a hero—an individual larger than ourselves who is capable of changing the course of history. How, we wonder, could Bob Geldof have done this by himself? What was happening around him and to him that made such action possible? In his own words, "Doors impenetrable a week earlier swung open effortlessly." Many of our good intentions seem to be smothered before we get off the couch. How were his efforts magnified and amplified?

In Brazil a multitude of interactions tipped a near tragedy into a triumph (at least for now). But who led, who followed and what were the obstacles and the opportunities for action? How did the effort of so many individuals produce the kind of results described above? Who were the individuals who contributed to this miracle?

This book answers those questions. This book is about figuring out how to make the impossible happen. It is about the "first light of evening" and about a world where ultimate good can be not only imagined, but also created. It assumes that in any social innovation something radically new occurs and assumes that, for this to happen, there must be, first and foremost, a belief that intractable problems can be solved. It assumes there must be an individual or group of individuals poised and ready to act—but these do not have to be perfect people. There must be an alignment of circumstances that make action possible. The trick is to see the relationship among all these elements. And in order to see, we must often change our thinking. We must move from seeing the world as simple, or even merely complicated. To understand social innovation we must see the world in all its complexity. In good measure, therefore, this is a book about how to think about complexity.

Traditional methods of seeing the world compare its workings to a machine. We say "things are working like clockwork" or "like a well-oiled machine," and people are seen as "human resources" who use management "tools." By using a machine metaphor, often unconsciously, we ignore the living aspects of our world and our work. Complexity science embraces life as it is: unpredictable, emergent, evolving and adaptable—not the least bit machine-like. And though it implies that even though we cannot control the world the way we can control a machine, we are not powerless, either. Using insights about *how the world is changed*, we can become active participants in shaping those changes.

All complex systems, from human beings to stock markets to global organizations, share behaviours that cannot be explained by their parts. The whole is different than the sum of the parts. You cannot fully understand a human body by describing it as a list of its parts, just as an organization chart barely scratches the surface in describing an organization. In complex systems, relationships are key. Connections or relationships define how complex systems work; an organization is its relationships not its flow chart. And this perception is crucial in understanding how complex systems differ from simple or complicated systems.

Yet we long for simple solutions to our complex social problems, are drawn to mechanical solutions that prescribe one-size-fits-all remedies and measurable results, and often feel that the circumstances we face—politically, culturally and personally—are too overwhelming for us to take any positive action to change them. The word "complex" applied to any situation can seem like a code word for inertia from our politicians and resignation as a citizen, but the revelations of complexity theory actually reveal the shock of the possible—a vivid term coined by Eric Young.

Some of the challenges we face as humans are as simple as they seem—like baking a cake. If we follow the recipe, measure properly and mix the ingredients in the right order, bring the oven to the right temperature and take the cake out when the timer dings, we have a reasonable chance of enjoying the result. Baking a cake has clear cause and effect relationships that can be mastered through developing and repeating basic skills. Even someone who has never baked still has a high probability of success since a well-tested cake recipe outlines the steps that have worked in the past and should continue to work in the future. Human systems designed around an assembly line have a similar "recipe" quality.

Everyone would agree that sending a rocket to the moon is not simple. Expertise is needed—and coordination of the experts is an area of expertise in itself. Formulas and the latest scientific evidence have to be applied to predict the trajectory and path of the rocket. Calculations are required to ensure the vessel carries sufficient fuel based on current conditions. This is a complicated problem, but if all specifications are met, all tests done, if the coordination and communication systems are sophisticated and functioning, and if everything is done in the right order, there is a high degree of certainty that we can control the outcome. Moreover, success in sending one rocket to the moon increases assurance that the next will also succeed.

Simple, Complicated and Complex Problems[4]

SIMPLE	COMPLICATED	COMPLEX
Baking a Cake	**Sending a Rocket to the Moon**	**Raising a Child**
The recipe is essential	Rigid protocols or formulas are needed	Rigid protocols have a limited application or are counter-productive
Recipes are tested to assure easy replication	Sending one rocket increases the likeli-hood that the next will also be a success	Raising one child provides experience but is no guarantee of success with the next
No particular expertise is required, but experience increases success rate	High levels of expertise and training in a variety of fields are necessary for success	Expertise helps but only when balanced with responsiveness to the particular child
A good recipe produces nearly the same cake every time	Key elements of each rocket MUST be identical to succeed	Every child is unique and must be understood as an individual
The best recipes give good results every time	There is a high degree of certainty of outcome	Uncertainty of outcome remains
A good recipe notes the quantity and nature of the "parts" needed and specifies the order in which to combine them, but there is room for experimentation	Success depends on a blueprint that directs both the development of separate parts and specifies the exact relationship in which to assemble them	Can't separate the parts from the whole; essence exists in the relationship between different people, differ-ent experiences, diff-erent moments in time

But parenting is complex. Unlike baking a cake or sending a rocket to the moon, there are no clear rules to follow to guarantee success. Every parent knows that raising one child provides experience but is no assurance of success with future children. And while parents often resort to reading the manuals written by experts, the texts all seem strangely inadequate. This is because every child is unique and must be understood as an individual. Moreover, the child evolves and changes in response to forces that parents do not control. The flour does not suddenly change its mind, and gravity can be counted on. Children, however, have minds of their own. Hence our interventions are always interactions. There are very few stand-alone parenting tasks. Almost always, the parents and child interact to create outcomes.

Successful social innovation combines all three problems—simple, complicated and complex—but the least understood is the complex. And yet complexity is the most fundamental level when we try to understand how social innovations occur. Both Live Aid and the Brazil HIV/AIDS miracle are the products of complex interaction. Single individuals, single actions and single organizations all play a part, but it is the subtle rules of engagement, between and among the elements, that is the force that seems to give initiatives a life of their own. In other words, complex systems comprise relationships. Relationships exist between things. You can point at things, but you can't point at relationships. They are literally hard to see.[5]

Disasters can occur when complex issues are managed or measured as if they are merely complicated or even simple. For example, our current approaches to dealing with mental illness focus on engineering the correct psycho-pharmaceutical intervention to fix the problem. The fact that many patients are too ill to adhere to their prescribed drug regimens is ignored as it demands of our specialists a level of interaction and adjustment most are not equipped to deliver. A new layer of expertise develops around forcing compliance to the drug regimens rather than crafting regimens and support systems that respond to the needs and circumstances of the patient.

Similarly, we organize our schools to be efficient in supplying education to large numbers and largely unresponsive to the wide range of learning styles and capacities that we know exists. Then we diagnose those who cannot learn efficiently as suffering from learning disorders and attempt to treat them, not the system.

Both of these are examples of addressing apparently intractable problems, crying out for social innovation, with methods, tools, approaches and mindsets that are appropriate for complicated situations. And while at times such an approach can give us a measure of false security, inevitably it gets us into trouble.

As the world has become more interrelated through global travel, disease transmission, population growth and migration, and global economic initiatives, our sense of being able to stay in control of the circumstances that most affect us diminishes. And as the illusion of control diminishes, we experience increased pace and intensity of change. We feel like we are in a vehicle hurtling to who-knows-where.

If we were to step off Earth and onto a larger planet like Jupiter, we would be acutely aware of gravity exerting a much greater force. Well, we are now in a time when complexity is exerting a much greater force. Our social and economic systems are undergoing a phase transition.[6] We no longer have the luxury of remaining complacent. As Francis Bacon pointed out four hundred years ago, "He that will not apply new remedies must expect new evils; for time is the greatest innovator." Time and the times are indeed presenting us with new challenges and opportunities on an unprecedented global scale.

As Eric Young has said: "We know two things with absolute certainty: (1) that in twenty years, even ten, our world will look very different, and (2) that the decisions and actions we take today will significantly shape our emergent future. However, we can have no certainty about what the future will be. It is not a good time for control freaks."[7]

But it is a good time for those capable of living with uncertainty. Times of great complexity offer the possibility of transformation. Those willing to embrace complexity are offered some immunity from the sense of "being stuck" that afflicts so many, from the feeling that the system can't be changed, that we have to accept famine, disease or war as inevitable.

—

Linda Lundström designs and manufactures women's clothes. Through her young adulthood, her focus had been on fashion, not an area where one thinks to look for a story of social change.[8]

In 1986, Lundström was at home breastfeeding her infant daughter one day. The baby was a bit fussy and taking longer than normal. To help pass the time, Lundström turned on the TV and saw John Kim Bell, an Aboriginal conductor and composer. He was talking about artistic talent in the First Nations community in Canada, and Lundström found herself mesmerized. Memories came flooding back of her childhood in Red Lake, a mining town in northern Ontario, and its racism toward First Nations. She began to cry and couldn't stop.

As a girl, she hadn't been particularly aware of the racism rampant in the town, and she'd left for good at seventeen. Yet she felt as if John Kim Bell was speaking directly to her, and that she must have been more aware of the racism than she had ever wanted to admit.

Entrepreneurs are competitive people, and Lundström is no exception. When she was fifteen, there was a competition in Red Lake and the surrounding communities to select a girl to represent the area. Whoever sold the most tickets to the Winter Carnival Dance would win a prize and become Winter Carnival Queen. Lundström desperately wanted to be the queen. Competition was tough and Red Lake was the smallest of the towns competing. She knew she would have to find an angle that others hadn't used in order to increase her sales.

The mining company had built and owned most of the houses in Red Lake. They all looked pretty much alike from the outside. But the First Nations people lived on one side of the mine and the whites lived on the other. Every day the First Nations children walked around the mine to go to school on the white side. Whites rarely crossed over to the Native side.

Lundström decided she would expand her market by selling to the First Nations people. Without telling her parents, she headed off to "Hiawatha Drive"—as the street where the First Nations community lived was derogatorily called by the whites. The first door was answered by a woman who was stunned to see a white girl standing there. Lundström was even more stunned to look over the woman's shoulder and into her house. There was no plumbing or electricity, and the walls were unfinished. As she went from door to door, she saw the same thing again and again. The mining company had put a roof over the First Nations employees to create the illusion that their treatment of all staff was equitable. But the houses were shells. Lundström sold tickets to every First Nations person who answered the door and became the Winter Carnival Queen, but not one Native person attended the dance.

As she watched John Kim Bell on television, Lundström felt like she was back on "Hiawatha Drive." But she was no longer a teenager; she was a successful businesswoman in her mid-thirties with influence. She couldn't believe that she had "forgotten" those early experiences. And the nagging feeling that she was part of the problem and hence had to be part of the solution stayed with her after the tears finally stopped. Over the next few days she realized that she needed to start somewhere. And, like Geldof, she knew intuitively that the best place for her to start was where she was. Geldof decided to reverse starvation the only way he could: by making a record. Lundström decided to reverse racism the only way she could: by starting a new line of clothing.

Lundström called John Kim Bell not only to offer a donation to his Native Arts Foundation (now the National Aboriginal Achievement Foundation), but to share her inspiration. They decided to have an ongoing art competition sponsored by Lundström. The winning artist's work would be used to embellish a line of coats fashioned after the traditional Inuit parka. Each coat sold with a Native motif would carry a card printed with the name of the artist along with his or her story about the meaning of the design.

Lundström also travelled back to Red Lake to meet the First Nations people in her hometown. She admired the beautiful beadwork of the women and asked if they would like to make beaded jewelry to complement her clothing lines. The women who met regularly to create beadwork for Lundström began to call themselves the Niichiikwewak (the Beadworkers). Although Lundström's goal was to provide them with an opportunity to earn income and establish a business, she was surprised at the significance of the social aspects of the Niichiikwewak beaders. The women in the beading business became a support group for each other, became more confident and developed a stronger collective voice.

As her own fashion business grew and thrived, Lundström found that people were interested in what she had to say. She was invited to give more speeches to community and business groups. She used these as opportunities to share her story of growing up in Red Lake and of her sense of calling to address racism and segregation. The more open and honest she was in her talks, the more she was invited to speak. Even when she was speaking to bankers on her latest business approach, she managed to find a way to raise the issue of racism in Canada.

With the honoraria for her speeches, she established the Kiishik Fund, a foundation whose aim is to educate children about First Nations heritage by bringing them into classrooms to share their language, art and traditions. The foundation also sends First Nations students into the bush with elders and teachers to learn the ways of their ancestors.

Lundström is neither a reader nor an intellectual, but she is a graduate of the school of life. Despite the fact that the accolades for her community work continue to pile up, including two honorary doctorates and many local and national awards for her contributions to building community, she would be the first to acknowledge that twenty years of activism have made only the smallest dent in the problem of racism.

Like Geldof, Lundström is an unlikely missionary. She believes that she acted not out of great confidence in her abilities but because she had no choice. To delay action further was to become a part of the system she saw as wrong. So she acted in a way that presented itself most immediately to her. She set out alone, with no guarantee that she would succeed. To her surprise, the response was warm. The First Nations craftswomen worked with her; the leaders supported her ideas; the ideas flowed. This is how social transformation happens.

—

When Rusty Pritchard and his wife, Joanna, had their first child, they made an unusual decision. Instead of fleeing to the suburbs of Atlanta, Georgia, where the streets are safe and the lawns are green, they bought a house in a slum in the inner city, renowned for its crack houses and prostitutes.[9]

Rusty was a professor at nearby Emory University, but he didn't move to the neighbourhood to do research. Rather, the choice was an act of faith, that by taking this risk he and Joanna could make a small contribution to transforming a neighbourhood.

The Pritchards were members of a liberal, progressive and evangelical group concerned with acting on the social justice implications of Christian faith. These were thoughtful, educated people. They were interested in writers like John Perkins and Bob Lupton, who were determined to rebuild the communities of American cities.[10] The Pritchards saw this process of transformation as one of great complexity, but one where even a small group of individuals working together could tip the dynamics of the system. They believed, for example that if a certain percentage of middle-class people moved to a neighbourhood, the violence and drug use in that neighbourhood would abate. This wouldn't be gradual. If X percent bought houses and moved in, nothing would happen; if $X + 1$ percent of the houses were owned by the middle class, there would be a sudden shift. Rusty and his wife were willing to be a drop in the bucket because they believed that when that bucket was full enough, it would tip, and the neighbourhood would be better not only for them but for many.

Rusty recalls: "There were families that moved there before us, or to nearby neighbourhoods. Four families in one place, three in another, two in another, a few more sprinkled around nearby. We were part of the second wave. Now there are eleven households—not all are families, some are single people who live together—in four neighbourhoods all in the southern part of Atlanta who meet together in a more organized way as a 'church' in a senior citizens' centre, who think very strategically about rebuilding community. There were, of course, a latent, disconnected body of long-term residents, homeowners, who weathered the bad years, persisting but staying behind burglar bars, who begin to re-emerge and provide the baseline fuel load for re-ignition of strong community." Rusty, Joanna and the other like-minded souls wanted to be the additional fuel and (importantly) the intentional spark to re-ignite the good social capital.

Research gave some support to their assumptions. Jonathan Crane from the University of Illinois studied changes in the rates of teen pregnancies and school dropouts across the United States, comparing communities with different proportions of high-status adults or role models, such as professionals, managers or teachers.[11] In communities where fewer than 5 percent were professionals, the number of teenage pregnancies and high school dropouts was high. But if the proportion of professionals passed the 5 percent threshold, the number of teen pregnancies and high school dropouts was dramatically lower. Like water becoming ice, the 5 percent level was a "phase transition threshold": a point at which a system transformation seems to occur. Adding more role models above the 5 percent level had very little impact on the results. But even a slight drop below the 5 percent level was enough to double the incidence of dropouts and teen pregnancies. This is what is referred to as the "tipping point," popularized by Malcolm Gladwell in his book of the same name.

Despite evidence from such studies and the company of others, what Rusty and Joanna Pritchard did required a leap of faith. This was, after all, not a research experiment, it was their lives. They believed engagement to be key—if this kind of sea change was to occur it would be through the ripple effects of changing neighbourhood interactions. After they moved in, Rusty looked around for a way to get involved. He noticed the kids in the neighbourhood had bicycles, but many were broken. He opened a bicycle repair clinic on Saturday mornings in his own driveway. Soon the kids were flocking to learn about bicycle repair. And this began to show results.

Some of the bike-repair club are now in high school and training as junior counsellors for a summer day camp Rusty's group started that reaches out to other neighbourhood children. Rusty says, "These young men and women are real leaders in caring for others! The bike-repair group became a miracle of sharing, as spare parts, tires, tubes and tube patches are accumulated and left behind for others."

This is a story in progress, a transformation underway. But that is one of the important things about social innovation; it is not a fixed address. By the time we arrive the destination has changed. So it takes perseverance as well as patience. No one, Rusty least of all, would glorify his act as in itself a social innovation, and yet, like the Brazil HIV/AIDS miracle, he is joining with many others who believe that, by doing their bit, they will be part of a transformation. He and his wife followed their conscience, but they were thinking like a movement. "What convinced us to give it a try?" Rusty says. "Quite simply . . . we couldn't do anything else. We'd been involved in social justice ministries in 'client/provider' relationships and found it very unsatisfying. We wanted to be part of a community and learn from people who were trying to live out the gospel of Christ with their whole lives, even if it didn't make a difference on the ground. Nobody in our group thinks we've arrived at answers, just that we've joined a community that keeps us asking the right questions."

This attitude is fundamental to a complexity perspective. Social innovation requires that while we may not be able to predict outcomes, certain kinds of interactions are more likely to result in transformation than others. Rusty and Joanna thought, acted and waited patiently. This is the way social innovation happens.

—

Our intention in writing this book is to connect with people who desire to make a difference. We can act only in time and space, we can act only from who we are. This apparent limitation is actually our greatest strength. In connecting to the world, even in the smallest ways, we engage its complexity and we begin to shift the pattern around us as we ourselves begin to shift. Social innovation begins where the individual and the system meet. It takes courage to engage and stay engaged; it takes courage to act in the absence of certainty and clarity. But to not engage, to not connect does not mean we protect ourselves from uncertainty. In a sense, as Bob Geldof and Linda Lundström both realized, to not engage simply reinforces the walls inside and outside us, and makes the future much less bright. On the other hand, by paying attention to how and when we engage, as did Rusty and Joanna Pritchard and the HIV/AIDS workers in Brazil, we do more than pull down a few walls: we engage with possibility, we engage with what may be. And seeming miracles become possible.

Notice that the previous paragraph opened with "Our intention in writing . . ." Social innovators *intend* to bring about change, to make a difference, to transform. But as we will explore in this book, they work in a world that is itself transforming, that is changing the innovator as he or she seeks to change the world. A complexity lens allows us to look at these interactions more closely. Control is replaced by a toleration of ambiguity and the "can-do" mentality of "making things happen" is modified by an attitude that is simultaneously visionary and responsive to the unpredictable unfolding of events. The successful social innovator is, intentionally or not, a part of the dynamics of transformation rather than the heroic figure leading the charge.

At first blush, this may not seem like much of a gain. We tend to prefer the image of the leader on the charging stallion to that of the sailor trying to navigate stormy seas. The leader on the stallion seems to be in control of his destiny, while the sailor has no chance of controlling a stormy sea. The sea is too powerful to overcome with force and too unpredictable to reliably anticipate. Instead, the sailor needs to be adept at reading the weather, understanding the patterns, reacting to changes and adjusting his sails. What, then, is to be gained by this change of perspective? Just this: a greater chance of actual success by being more closely attuned to and aligned with how social innovation actually unfolds in the real world.

Many of the popular images and metaphors of complexity science emphasize rampant unpredictability and swirling chaos, as with hurricanes and tsunamis. A sense of helplessness, even fatalism, pervades many complexity models, suggesting we can know what has happened only after it has happened, and the exact same thing will never happen again. So why bother even figuring out what just happened? Complexity scientists believe they can portray real-world dynamics better than simple causal models, but they tend to downplay, even dismiss, the possibility of human agency. We, on the other hand, by studying successful social innovations and drawing on our own experiences, believe that social activists can use the insights that come from complexity theory to increase the likelihood of success. Not guarantee success. There are no guarantees, no certainties. This book does not promise success if you follow seven proven steps. Instead, we're about tipping the scales in favour of successful social innovations in the face of seemingly overwhelming odds. Getting to maybe—as our title suggests.

These two perspectives—intentionality and complexity—meet in tension. If you intend to do something, you make a deliberate commitment to act to bring about change. Complexity science is about unpredictable emergence without regard for (indeed, even in spite of) human intentions. These two perspectives meet in the question that is the foundation of this book: to what extent and in what ways can we be deliberate and intentional about those things that seem to emerge without our control, without our intention?

As we start on this journey, what can guide us? Here are a few points of orientation:

- **Questions are key.** In complex situations there are no final answers. But certain key questions illuminate the issues of social innovation.
- **Tensions and ambiguities are revealed through questioning.** Social innovation both reveals and creates tensions. Once understood, these tensions can then be engaged—not simply managed—in the interests of amplifying the desired change.
- **Relationships are key to understanding and engaging with the complex dynamics of social innovation.** For social innovation to succeed, everyone involved plays a role. As systems shift, everyone—funders, policy makers,

social innovators, volunteers, evaluators—is affected. It is what happens between people, organizations, communities and parts of systems that matters—"in the between" of relationships.

- **A certain mindset is crucial:** framed by inquiry not certitude, one that embraces paradoxes and tolerates multiple perspectives.

Questions, tensions, uncertainties, relationships, mindset. These words are a curiously reflective description of what, surely, is all about action. Doesn't innovation by definition require action? If Geldof, Lundström, the Pritchards and the legions of Brazilian HIV/AIDS workers had merely reflected, we wouldn't call it innovation. Or would we?

We've been taught that thinking is separate from doing. But in this book we offer thinking as a form of doing, and emphasize doing as an opportunity for thinking, reflecting and learning. Complexity science suggests that how we think about things matters. A fundamental sociological premise is the Thomas theorem: *what is perceived as real is real in its consequences.* We would add: *how we think about and understand the world frames our actions.* Indeed, we can be even more basic: *whether we think about things matters.*

The capacity to think astutely is often undervalued in the world of action. But philosopher Hannah Arendt identified the capacity to think as the foundation of a healthy and resilient democracy. Having experienced totalitarianism in Nazi Germany, then having fled it, she devoted much of her life to studying it and its opposite, democracy. She believed that thinking thoughtfully in public deliberations and acting democratically were intertwined and that totalitarianism is built on and sustained by deceit and thought control. In order to resist efforts by the powerful to deceive and control thinking, Arendt believed that people needed to practise thinking. She wrote that "experience in thinking . . . can be won, like all experience in doing something, only through practice, through exercises."[12]

We consider every effort at social innovation an opportunity for those involved to practise thinking.

Recent action on the world stage of politics offers a prime example. The American invasion of Iraq was conceived as a complicated problem with the goal of regime change. The U.S. military planned the invasion based on a "shock and awe" strategy, which would use overwhelmingly superior force and unprecedented speed to quash the Iraqi military. While there were some relatively minor deviations from the original plan, on the whole the invasion unfolded as an exercise in implementing a complicated blueprint for victory. "Mission accomplished," President George W. Bush declared. It worked, as far as it went. But then came the challenge of securing the peace.

Nation building is a complex challenge, more like rearing a child than sending a rocket to the moon. However, the United States in Iraq treated the tasks of securing the peace, instituting democracy and building a new nation as a complicated rather than complex problem. Perhaps the political environment and the controversy over the invasion kept those nominally "in charge" from being able to acknowledge their lack of control, the inherent uncertainties, rapidly changing and unstable system dynamics, and unpredictably emergent insurgencies. But we'd argue that failing to think about the situation as a complex rather than merely complicated problem has increased the chaos in Iraq and contributed to instability and loss of life. This is not a political judgment; this is a complexity judgment.

Our book's title riffs on the certitudes of a very popular management book about negotiations called *Getting to Yes*.[13] We think that getting to maybe is the best we can do, and we mean that in the best possible way. Just as social innovation holds thought and action in tension, and complexity theory, as we parse it, balances intention and unpredictability, the word "maybe" combines two ideas and holds them in tension.

MAY—possibility, what might be, the essence of intentionality as a vision of what could happen, if only . . .
BE—state of being, the way things are, presence, reality . . .

Getting to Maybe is about acting deliberately and intentionally in a complex, uncertain world by virtue of being in and of that world. For, as the social innovators we chronicle climb each mountain of maybe and reach the summit of realized possibility, a new mountain of maybe inevitably becomes visible in the distance. But we're getting ahead of ourselves. First we want to give you a preview of the journey itself—the journey that is the story of this book.

The examples we studied, through multiple conversations with social innovators in most cases and careful study of autobiographies in others, revealed an archetypal narrative that goes something like this. Some active, caring person becomes increasingly distressed by some problem (HIV/AIDS), injustice (racism) or situation (gang violence). That person decides that something must be done. The impossibility of things staying as they are gives birth to the possibility of change—what we've called getting to maybe—and that moment of recognition and birth is the focus of the next chapter.

By determining to take action this person becomes what we've come to call a social innovator. Our cases suggest that those who are ultimately successful begin their journey by more fully understanding the situation and the system that is the source of their discontent. They first "stand still" (see Chapter 3). As they observe, think, analyze, ponder, they also act. They look at where they are, who they are, where they might find allies and what scope of change is needed, and in so doing, they encounter the entrenched powers that benefit from and hold in place the existing system—the very system they want to change. That encounter with "powerful strangers" (Chapter 4) helps them discover, reframe and unlock critical resources.

The pace of the narrative picks up, often dramatically, as our social innovators find themselves in flow, in sync with others, moving rapidly forward in unexpected and unpredictable, even previously unimaginable ways. They thought they were looking for something and suddenly find that it has found them ("Let It Find You," Chapter 5). "Maybe" suddenly has the feel of "will be" or "must be."

But remember, this is a story of nonlinear dynamics and the unexpected— it does not unfold smoothly. New barriers emerge. Threatened powers fight back, for they too see what may be coming, and they don't like it. Resistance is aroused. Things start falling apart. The premise that things will likely get worse before they get better becomes fact, not theory. Doubt surfaces, grows, overwhelms—well, almost. It certainly feels that way. In this phase of the journey, the social innovator has descended unsuspecting into "cold heaven" (Chapter 6).

Then, sometimes at the darkest moment (this is an archetypal narrative after all), "hope and history rhyme" (Chapter 7). What seemed like a local, personal social quest suddenly connects with larger forces. It turns out that the timing is right, the moment has come, not through planning, not through rational goal setting, not through careful management and

forceful control, but by being at the right place at the right time:
a historical moment made conscious and intentional (not simply
accidental or serendipitous) by the prepared mind. Intentionality joins
possibility joins historical forces and becomes, in the words of poet
Seamus Heaney, "the outcry and the birth-cry of new life at its term."
In our words, social innovation has succeeded.

Looking back, the social innovator has a sense that a door opened—
however briefly ("The Door Opens," Chapter 8). At the beginning there
could be no certainty that the door would open. Still, it opened. Knowing
it had opened, seeing it open, having the will to move through it was
made possible by intentionality, the consciousness that comes from
paying attention to real-world dynamics, and the vision of the possible.

That's the storyline, the journey this book invites you to take. It is a story
in which there are no simple answers. No hero could take credit for the
outcomes. Yet this book is filled with heroic actions.

Yes, a dandelion
because they are the flower
of wishes. You blow that ball
of seeds and the wind carries them to the one
assigned to grant or reject.
And it's a good thing
that it's the dandelions
who have this power
because they are tough
and sometimes you have to be tough
to even remember
that you have any desires left at all,
to believe that even one
could be satisfied, would not turn
to an example of
"be careful what you wish for,
it might come true."
Maybe that's exactly why
there are so many of them—
the universe gives us extra chances
to keep dreaming.
Each one an uprising,
a burst of color
in the cracks of our hearts,
sunrise
at an unexpected time,
in an unexpected place.

Ellie Schoenfeld, "Lucien's Birthday Poem"

2. Getting to Maybe

Most of us have been struck at some time with the sense that things are not right with the world. It could be while watching a television show, or walking down the street on a cold winter day, or reading a newspaper, or talking to a friend. We think, "How is it possible, in this day and age, that women are being beaten to death, children are homeless, millions are starving?" We experience a sharp frustration. "I wish I could change things," we say to ourselves. But this wish is often followed by despair. "Who am I to make a difference? And anyway, what do I understand about this? The forces that keep the poor impoverished, the starving hungry are huge! Where would I even start? Wouldn't I have to change everything to change anything?" In the face of this overwhelming sense of *im*possibility, how do social transformations begin? How do social innovators connect to a sense of possibility in the face of the bad news that constantly fills our newspapers and TV screens?

—

Between 1990 and 1997, the number of youth homicides in the city of Boston fell from a high of ninety-seven to an all-time low of fifteen, a drop of some 60 percent. A shift of this magnitude was so extraordinary that in March 2000, an article appeared in the *New York Times* describing the city's remarkable success at eradicating youth violence as the "Boston miracle."

What happened in those seven years? The story is a complex one, involving many strands of circumstance and the weaving together of many dreams. But it is possible to track the threads of those dreams back to a small group of people who were drawn or dragged into a determined effort to create change. Key to the miracle were the actions of four ministers who joined forces to try to do something about young men who were killing each other. To look more closely at the story of one of those ministers, Reverend Jeff Brown, is instructive.

When Brown was a young divinity student, his dreams were pretty straightforward. He wanted to build his own church and increase his congregation. He dreamed of owning a nice car and buying a nice house in the suburbs for his family.[1] In 1987 he became the pastor of the Union Baptist Church, in Cambridge, Massachusetts. He got the nice house in the suburbs and the car, but his dream was far from realized. His congregation was in Boston's inner city, where youth homicide and violence were at their peak, and crack cocaine and gang warfare were everyday realities. Brown was appalled by this, and his first response was to improve the eloquence of his sermons. "Every Sunday, I would make a very eloquent sermon exhorting people to fight against the violence. By the late 1980s, I was really becoming very good at delivering powerful sermons. I was the rapping reverend," he says.

Brown, like others who lived or worked in the community, was deeply frustrated with the Boston police, who denied the existence of drug and gang problems.[2] By 1990, parents in Brown's parish, and other inner-city neighbourhoods, would not let their children play outside. Things kept getting worse. The streets were owned by gangs, drugs and guns. And still the police did not appear to be responding.

The force predominantly comprised white Irish Catholic men, and the distrust between the black community and the police was significant.[3] The distrust was heightened by the police department's "stop and search" or "stop and frisk" policy, introduced in May 1989 in an attempt to slow the escalation of violence. The community felt that the policy was implemented discriminately; if you were black you were always suspect. But the police themselves felt helpless in the face of the ever-increasing violence. No probation officers dared to roam the streets to see whether or not their charges were respecting their parole conditions, so gang youths were left to their own devices.

Brown's sermons were clearly not working, but he wasn't certain what to try instead. His own circumstances were getting to him. "The violence was all around my church and yet every night I would get into my car, drive by the gangs in the streets, and go home to my nice suburban house and my nice family," he remembers. Then one evening he attended a public lecture on city violence and was appalled by what he heard. The "trigger," he recalls, "was this woman who argued that we needed to write off this generation and focus on the next one. And I realized that by ignoring this generation we are dooming the next one. The next generation will have children from the generation we are willing to sacrifice. Who will take care of the next generation?"

Who indeed?

Shortly after that lecture, a boy Brown knew well was murdered because another kid wanted his jacket. At that moment Brown reached his own personal tipping point. It was time to stop hesitating and time to stop sermonizing. It was time to act.

The conviction seemed to reach out and grab him, and it didn't feel like a choice. Joseph Campbell writes about the experience of people whom history has treated as heroes. He suggests that at the beginning of their journey they receive a call: a strong signal from the world that they can't ignore. The operative word is "can't." Those who try to resist often find that events literally pull them, kicking and screaming, over a threshold into what becomes a terrific struggle, more of a nightmare than a dream. The only way out is to get through it. Brown described his own call in similar terms. He knew the youths wouldn't come in to him. He had to go out to them. It was a terrifying idea.

As he was gathering courage, another attack pushed him into the fray. A funeral was held in Morning Star Baptist Church for a young gang member gunned down in a drive-by shooting. As one of his friends, Jerome Brunson, entered the church to pay his respects, rival gang members followed Brunson inside, and beat him and stabbed him several times at the altar in front of scared and stunned mourners.[4] This became known as the Morning Star incident. The religious community was outraged, and suddenly Brown found he wasn't alone.

The religious leaders of the various congregations of different faiths in the Boston area called a press conference and denounced the Morning Star incident, gang violence and youth homicide. Then they called for all religious groups to meet and find a way to deal with the problem of violence. About three hundred clergy responded and, among these, Brown found companions. A group of clergy including Brown, Ray

Hammond, Eugene Rivers and about nine others formed a "street committee." Their goal was to be on the street and connect with gang members—to meet the violence face to face. Brown says, "We wanted [the street committee] to experience what was out there. . . . We agreed that the best action was to go out on the streets and see what was truly happening and learn from the kids and about the kids."

They decided that every Friday, from midnight to 4 a.m., the members of the street committee would go out in the neighbourhood and just walk around. Brown described this intrusion on gang territory as a collision of two worlds: the world of the people who had abandoned the streets for their safe world in the suburbs, and the world of the youths who lived and died on them.

The initial street walks were frightening excursions into a world of darkness and potential violence, a world Brown and the other ministers had studiously avoided in the past. The first few times nothing happened except long hours of being scared. The kids did not approach the group of ministers; they just watched. Then, about six weeks into the effort, the committee started seeing subtle changes. Brown is not sure what triggered the softening. "Perhaps we passed some test," he says. "Perhaps the gang members realized that we did not want anything from them, we just wanted to learn about them."

The gangs watched the ministers; the ministers watched the gangs. And slowly their perceptions began to shift. Brown and the others saw the network of connections within the gangs. Each gang was like a family; they stuck together and protected each other like a family. The individual members of the street committee started to reassess some of their biases concerning the gang members. All of the gang members came from poor families or drug-addicted parents. Perhaps the gang was the new-found family. Gradually, as the ministers' perceptions shifted, they began to see the gang members as kids creating and defending their own families. Not so different, come to think of it, from the ministers themselves.

Then one night, as they walked on the street, one of the kids took Ray Hammond to one side. As the committee members stood there, not listening but trying to ensure nothing happened to Hammond, this kid told him that with the things he had been doing, he seemed to have lost his soul. He asked Hammond if he could help him find it again. This was a pivotal moment.

Brown had bought into the myth that these kids were not religious, that they were materialistic and unemotional. But it was becoming clear to him and the others that this was not the case, and the divide he had drawn between himself and the gang kids finally crumbled. Like him, these kids wanted a nice car, shoes and brand-name pants. Like him, they wanted a family, and would defend that family to the death. And, like him, they also wanted a more meaningful life. At the end of the night, Brown realized, the kids and he were not that different.

The ministers walked every Friday night with the gang kids. During the weekends the ministers discussed their feelings among themselves. The process became nearly obsessive; they found themselves calling each other at all hours to hash over the events of the previous day, to make sense of what they were seeing. They reached out to include other groups in the community, like the police, lawyers, the juvenile court system. They explored and found commonalities. Ultimately, they began to see a way through: they called it the TenPoint Coalition.[5]

"We changed . . . I changed . . ." Brown's words reflect a pattern that seems to characterize social innovation, revealing the paradox that wanting to change others means accepting a profound change in oneself. There is a sense of co-evolution, of being "of the system" and never truly outside it. Self-reflection and self-revelation are necessary. For Brown this meant that he had to recognize his kinship to the gang members if he expected them to be open to a relationship with him. He could influence others but not control them. He needed to be part of the process, be a full participant in the changes. He learned that he had to resist the seduction of believing he was in control of the interactions, of the changes both in himself and in others.

—

For social innovators, like Jeff Brown, things often get worse before they get better. But the deep desire to change things, the call to try to make a difference, remains strong. The Boston initiative changed many times, as events and people joined and shaped its direction. But what kept them going, what became "nearly obsessive," was the strong feeling that something had to change and that they were the ones who must lead the way, not necessarily because they were the best people to do it but because they were the ones who realized it had to be done.

When Bob Geldof, in the midst of a frustrating recording contract negotiation, happened to switch on the television to see the starving children in Ethiopia, his reaction was intense. "I felt disgusted, enraged and outraged, but more than all those, I felt deep shame," he writes. "A horror like this could not have happened without our consent. We had allowed this to happen and now we knew it was happening, to allow it to continue would be tantamount to murder . . . To expiate yourself truly of any complicity in this evil meant you had to give something of yourself. I was stood against the wall. I had to withdraw my consent."[6]

The *Oxford English Dictionary* defines the noun "calling" as "the inward feeling or conviction of a divine call; the strong impulse to any course of action as the right thing to do." The idea of a calling was originally connected to a religious vocation, and in fact, many social innovators we encountered were deeply religious. Those who weren't nonetheless seemed to be propelled by a value system they couldn't ignore or dismiss. Getting to maybe is certainly a calling. Jeff Brown felt it, Bob Geldof felt it, Linda Lundström felt it. "It" wasn't a tentative invitation, but rather a violent yank over the threshold into an arena that was surprising, unpleasant, even frightening, but unavoidable.

Calls come in different ways to different people. But all who are called sense that action is not optional; it is essential, a necessity for the survival of self. For some, the call becomes a long-term act of devotion, a weaving of identity and destiny, an effort to combine what they most love and believe in with what they do in the world. Poet Robert Frost writes, "My object in living is to unite / My avocation and my vocation / As my two eyes make one in sight."[7] For others the call is born of the emergency of the moment: a crisis appearing and requiring an instant action in response. This is the individual who courageously rescues someone from a burning building and then claims that anyone would have done the same.

Our cases are somewhat different. The calling for these social innovators is a long-term, sustained endeavour. For Brown, the initial calling may have been his vocation in the ministry. For a time he tried to make that suffice. But the crisis of escalating violence called him in a different kind of way, forcing him to the conviction that he needed to change what he was doing. Even then, it took courage to go out onto the streets—but it seemed the only way. And last came his perseverance, the sticking to what he and the other ministers had started, the insistence on seeing it through. The calling was in itself complex, a combination of inner and outer callings, needing both short- and long-term involvement. Social innovation takes conviction and courage, and it also takes devotion, of the more sustained kind we often think of as perseverance.

Jeff Brown's story suggests that a calling occurs when we see something that we feel is wrong. We can ignore the calling, or we can respond to it, but we shouldn't ignore it because we feel that we are alone. The fact that we see the problem or hear the call may well signal a readiness for change in the system. One of the signs of that readiness in this instance is the surprising impact the call had on the system. After the Morning Star incident, Brown felt moved to action, and to his surprise he found that he was not alone. This is an experience echoed over and over again in the stories of social innovators.

Complexity theory can offer us some insights into this phenomenon. While there is no doubt that social innovators like Jeff Brown and Bob Geldof are leaders in that they initiate change, it is also clear that their first, tentative steps were not part of some grand strategy, but rather experiments they felt compelled by circumstance to try. Often to their own surprise, the response to their initiatives was not only positive, but also as if they had catalyzed a chemical reaction: the system seemed to shift in ways they had never imagined. Complexity theory would suggest that the reason for their success was not so much that they led the troops like generals on their horses, but rather that their responses both epitomized and provoked a new pattern of interactions. In short, that they were both creating and reinforcing a "strange attractor."

The idea of an attractor is an old one, key to many scientific theories. Attractors hold a system in its current pattern or propel it to a new pattern. They are the stable factors within system dynamics. They represent the general trend of a system around which the details congregate.

Different kinds of attractors exist. For example, a magnet held over a dish of paper clips is a single-point attractor. The paper clips are pulled toward the same point—the magnet. A group of people trying to push a car out of the mud are all directing their energy toward a single point. Sailors on a boat will work together to reach a visible shore. It is in this context that the idea of the hero has traditionally found its support: the single, lone leader who is master of the craft and who directs all others to that single end.

An attractor may be periodic or oscillate back and forth between two points. A heart rate has a natural rhythm that is periodic. The heart pumps and rests, pumps and rests. Breathing is a natural pattern of oscillation between inhaling and exhaling; we can predict that an inhalation will follow an exhalation. Seasonality in a business may be a periodic attractor. Cash flow in seasonal businesses is a bit like the breathing rhythm—there is a time for spending cash followed by a time for collecting cash. Again, for those involved, the goals produce a clarity that allows them to switch their behaviour in a synchronized fashion. If the winds are not behind them, the sailors may have to tack back and forth to reach the shore. All the more reason for a heroic leader who can anticipate the changes.

However, in a now famous discovery in the 1960s, Edward Lorenz unlocked the puzzle of weather patterns and established a third kind of attractor, the strange attractor.[8] How many times have you overheard someone ask, "Why can't the weather forecaster get it right?" The assumption in this question is that with sufficient data, weather should be predictable with a high degree of accuracy. But it isn't. Nonetheless the weather demonstrates patterns that are not random in spite of eluding accurate prediction. When Lorenz fed a few interacting non-linear equations fashioned after observed weather data into a computer simulation, he found that the computer generated a pattern with a recognizable shape, like a three-dimensional pair of butterfly wings. While the weather seen from any particular locale had little predictable pattern, at this global level a distinct pattern could be observed. This pattern could not be explained by a single variable (point attractor) or by an oscillation (periodic attractor). It was clear that an attractor or force was at work but it was difficult to identify, hence strange. Lorenz's simulation showed that even minor differences affected the path of an individual weather trajectory, confounding the ability of observers to predict or forecast any particular weather event. However, some

underlying rules or dynamics, which together formed the strange attractor, kept the overall pattern recognizable. The exact nature of the strange attractor remained obscure.

Craig Reynolds wasn't afraid to hunt for the rules shaping complex systems, and he also used computer simulations to help him. He noticed that the pattern birds, fish and bees adopted when flocking also had similarities to the weather. The exact flight path of any bird, or even of the whole flock, was difficult to predict, but the overall pattern wasn't; it seemed to be regulated by some underlying dynamic or strange attractor. Ask a group of people if they have ever had a bird fly into the window of their home or office, and inevitably almost all will say they have. Ask them if they have ever seen a flock of birds fly into a window, and the usual response is no. Then ask them why. Most people will be a bit stymied by this line of inquiry.

Many are awestruck when they are told that a flock of birds, a school of fish or a hive of bees is up to fifty times more sensitive to changes in its environment than any single bird, fish or bee. In other words, they can respond to stimuli, like predators or windows, much more readily in this group formation than when they are on their own.

What gives the group this ultra-sensitivity? Reynolds was curious about this and knew that it couldn't be explained by looking at the parts alone. The individual bird as heroic leader is a highly improbable explanation. Hence he decided to simulate this behaviour by looking at the rules of interaction that allowed the birds (or "boids," as he called their simulated counterparts) to be more sensitive to stimuli and changes in their environment. Through trial and error, Reynolds finally settled on three simple rules of interaction. (He discovered that if he put in more than three rules, his boids became less sensitive. There seemed to be a minimum and critical number of rules, beyond which rules inhibited sensitivity.) Strange attractors, while often a feature of complex systems, do not in themselves need to be complex—indeed they can be as breathtakingly simple as

1. Maintain a minimum distance with other boids and objects (such as windows).
2. Maintain the same speed as neighbouring boids (measured in three dimensions around the boid).
3. Head toward the centre of the flock.

All three must be operational at all times. For example, if only rule three was observed, disaster would ensue. With all three in place, Reynolds's boids move with a fluid motion that looks remarkably like a flock of starlings in flight.

You can try this with a group of people. In a large space, ask each group member to do three things: (1) find two "reference" people whom she will secretly keep in her sights for the next few minutes, (2) begin and keep moving around the space without bumping into anyone else and (3) try to stay equidistant from the two reference people. As everyone does this, someone watching from a balcony above will see a pattern reminiscent of flocking birds, although the people involved may not be aware of the pattern.

Even more interesting, now pick two people and tell them quietly that, while continuing to keep equidistant from their reference people, they should gradually move toward and out the door. In as little as sixty seconds the entire group will have swarmed out of the room. This is a dramatic example of how patterns are driven by simple rules.

So complex systems are shaped by strange attractors that may turn out to be governed by very simple rules. Unfortunately, such simple rules are not written down in a rule book for social innovators! Although some simple rules are very resilient, in both nature and human systems the rules can also change and evolve.

—

How do social innovators determine the rules that perpetuate a negative pattern such as youth homicide? Craig Reynolds developed a sense of the whole system through a computer simulation, but sometimes careful observation and thoughtful analysis of small interactions around us can be equally revealing. One characteristic of strange attractors is "scalar invariance." In other words, at each scale from very small (a few birds) to very large (a huge migrating flock) the rules, and hence the dynamics, remain the same. In essence, you can see the whole in the parts.

Lorenz's weather pattern exhibited this trait. Whether he plotted the data for a week or a year, the 3-D butterfly shape was still visible. In human systems, too, we can tell when a system is being influenced by a strange attractor: disparate parts apparently not linked in time or space start to follow a similar pattern or shape. For example, we travel on an airplane and we notice that the flight attendant who serves us is frowning. When we make a simple request, she snaps at us. We look to see if she is the only flight attendant behaving this way, and notice that the whole crew seems cranky, no happier with each other than they are with the passengers. If we ask a friend who works for the airline what is going on, she tells us that the airline is in trouble, that they have been cutting perks to staff in the interest of controlling costs. When we ask about why the airline is in trouble, we discover that the whole industry is suffering from similar challenges. The behaviour we see on the plane is symptomatic of the larger system dynamic. At every level we see stress, unhappiness, failure to collaborate, and failure to find out how to break the vicious cycle.

In the aftermath of Hurricane Katrina, many Americans had an experience of scalar invariance. When they saw the pictures on television, many people were struck with how much New Orleans looked like a developing country's disaster zone—Indonesia, perhaps, or Somalia. How shocking that such images should come from an American city, a tourist destination renowned for its music and festivals. And yet the disaster was a manifestation, on a local scale, of a set of economic rules and interactions that have been driving economic growth and environmental degradation at a global scale for decades. The policies that directed investment away from the repair of the levees in New

Orleans, away from the protection and restoration of the wetlands that provide coastal protection to that city, were embedded in a broader economic philosophy that legitimizes treating most natural and some human resources as free and therefore fails to account for the full cost of resources needed to maintain economic growth rates. This failure is often termed "externalizing costs." At the global scale these economic philosophies are the same ones that externalize the costs of emissions of CO_2 by manufacturers in the industrial North, contributing both to global warming and to deaths in the developing South.[9] It is the same economic system that puts economic growth ahead of environmental protection at every level from local to global. It is the same economic system that builds wealth on the interest paid by the poor on their debts, whether on developing countries' debt or the credit card debt of the poor in the developed world.

The rich can escape the environmental disasters that are to some extent the results of the economic activity that made them rich; the poor cannot escape. And the poor are often black, whether in Africa or in the United States. It was no accident that the images from Katrina resembled those from Somalia.

—

Many social innovators are adept at seeing such patterns in the interactions around them. Just as a diviner with a willow rod can find water, a social innovator can home in on key simple rules and move to intervene. Bob Geldof saw a breakdown in connections between the disaffected youth who "consumed" rock music and the dispossessed hungry in Ethiopia and Sudan who had nothing to eat; between those who wanted to help, including NGOs inhibited by cumbersome bureaucracy, and those who needed that help. He moved instinctively to rearrange those relationships—change those rules. At first he didn't have a clear sense of what to do or how to do it, and he had *no* certainty as to outcome. This is important to remember, because certainty is rare among social innovators. Rather, as we have tried to capture with the idea of calling, the spur to action is more often a compelling juxtaposition of opportunity and conviction. And as we have seen in our story of Jeff Brown, action takes courage.

Jeff Brown and the other ministers were part of the system they tried to transform. They initially reinforced the set of rules and interactions that governed community relationships where they lived. These included a rule of separation—there is a difference between the street gangs and most of us; a rule of avoidance—the streets are dangerous places from which we must take refuge; and a rule of intolerance—we can condemn the violence but not understand it.

A whole series of events, of policies, of reinforcing stereotypes worked to hold this system within a defined, bounded reality. The patterns were repeated night after night. It came to be no surprise to read in the morning papers of yet another gang-related murder, of another young black man under arrest, of another more stringent anti-crime policy.

Fear of the enemy was a profound factor in holding the pattern together. The sides in the dispute were seen as opposites with nothing in common: black and white, youth and middle-aged, unemployed and employed, evil and good, dangerous and safe, and so on. This strange attractor held the city together in a dangerous dance.

The change in Boston began by changing these basic rules. Despite their own fear and mistrust, the ministers felt they needed to be true to their values. They decided that they would go out on the street, they would assume that gang members were not completely different from themselves and that, therefore, they could understand the violence as well as condemn it. They acted from faith and intuition. And on a local scale they began to change the rules that held the vicious cycle of fear in place.

What is interesting about the Boston case, and key in understanding how to get to maybe, is the fact that as the interactions between gang members and ministers began to reshape their relationships and identities, similar things were happening on a broader scale throughout the city. Revelations of corruption in the police department eroded the idea of the police as moral enforcers. The "stop and frisk" policies began to give way to more measured interactions. Individuals and groups began to reconnect and to rethink their identities. Once seen as opposites, the two sides realized they shared some significant attributes: extreme group loyalty and protectionism (youth gangs, ministers and police alike). Key assumptions about the differences between the groups began to erode. The adversarial positions didn't totally disappear, but people found that not everything was about difference, about being on opposite sides. Throughout the city, hope began to replace fear. And the murder rate kept dropping.

Does this mean that if Jeff Brown and his colleagues had not stepped into the streets, the system would have reconfigured anyway? In complex systems, attributing praise and blame is tricky. When Brown and his colleagues took action, remember, it didn't feel like a choice; it was a call they had to answer. Few would deny the importance of their actions in shifting the local system in important ways. But their actions had power partly because the system was ready to move. Which snowflake breaks the branch?

This is one of the paradoxes at the heart of successful social innovation: we are not free from the responsibility to act in accordance with our calling, yet we should not claim either full credit or full responsibility for the results of our actions. This chapter began with a poem that spoke of dandelions as "the flower / of wishes. You blow that ball / of seeds and the wind carries them to the one / assigned to grant or reject." Even experienced social innovators often speak, like the poet does, of their deep surprise when their actions seem aligned with transforming results. They dream that something is possible, they "blow that ball of seeds" and find, sometimes, that there is "an uprising, / a burst of color / in the cracks of our hearts, / sunrise / at an unexpected time, / in an unexpected place." We don't stand outside the complex system we are trying to change: when it changes, we do; when we change, it does. Getting to maybe has almost nothing to do with certainty and everything to do with serendipity, conviction, risk taking and faith.

How to Get to Maybe

We began this chapter with two key questions. How do social transformations begin? And how do social innovators connect to possibility?

Using the idea of calling, the strange attractor metaphor and the simple rules concept, we looked at our cases for insights into these questions. Strange attractors are held together by paradoxes. Our stories reveal a few of these paradoxes: profound uncertainty and deep understanding, self-protection and vulnerability, and changing others by changing oneself.

But for those of us who want to make a change in the system, how do we take those first steps? In the last chapter we suggested that the only place to start was where one was. Some of us are students, some of us caring community members; some work in government, some in philanthropic foundations, some in voluntary-sector organizations, still others in corporations. If we are to get to maybe, to answer our call and to connect with the possibility for change, we may need to start doing things a little differently.

Let's imagine the example of an experienced leader of a major philanthropic foundation. The philanthropist and her trustees have recently completed a strategic review of the foundation's mission and have decided they want to support significant social innovation, but aren't sure how to do it. Given the chance for a conversation, here's what we might tell her.

• Support vision, people with a strong sense of calling, and emergent possibilities.

Why this advice in particular? Because the funding community in North America has fallen under the enchantment of measurable outcomes. Most foundations will consider only proposals with clear, specific and measurable outcomes. Such an approach is appropriate when problems are well understood and solutions are known. But for the complex problems that social innovators address, an equally innovative funding approach is required. Perhaps funders should be looking to support people, not projects. Don't expect clarity, which in these early stages of exploration is inappropriate. But do expect a strong and passionate sense of calling and an emphasis on changing the rules of interaction. This is risky—true venture philanthropy—and it's a way to support genuine social innovation.

• Support intense interactions, networking and information exchange among those who have the potential to tip a system in a new direction.

Remember that Jeff Brown was empowered to act by finding that he wasn't alone. Convening people who are concerned about a social problem, particularly in a timely and flexible way, can begin a sea change. Crisis creates opportunity, but our governments may not be flexible enough to respond. As a funder, you can add resources to an emerging system quickly and flexibly.

• Remove barriers to innovation.

Social innovators don't look to government to make things happen. *Social innovators* make things happen. Social innovators worry about overcoming regulatory and policy barriers that support the status quo, impose controls and sap energy. We'd want to work with the public sector to identify, map and examine system barriers, including barriers erected by government. In many cases a solution adopted by government to solve some earlier problem becomes, over time, itself a problem. A simple, classic example is installing traffic lights at intersections where there have been fatal automobile accidents. Over time, so many traffic lights are added that traffic is significantly slowed and frustrated motorists start running red lights, causing new accidents. Removing barriers to facilitate new interactions can be an important contribution to sparking social innovation.

One of the barriers we often see in not-for-profit organizations is what the media calls "compassion fatigue." What would we tell the director of a voluntary organization, an organization whose members have been battling the illness, poverty, violence or fear that seems to be always with us?

First, it strikes us that voluntary-sector organizations have become embarrassed by real emotion and genuine passion as they have become more professional. Dependent on government funding, many voluntary-sector organizations have become overly cautious. Part of their challenge is to find the courage to articulate the vision that can rekindle the flame.

We've facilitated sessions where seasoned voluntary-sector leaders are asked to recall and express what originally brought them to their work. It wasn't the great opportunities offered to write stilted proposals to capture government funding. It was because they cared, and cared deeply, about the homeless, child victims of abuse, community violence or some other problem—and they wanted to make a difference. Effective and innovative organizations keep alive that vision and passion, that sense of calling.

• Speak passionately about the things that really matter to you. Give voice to those you serve who live the problems you want to attack.

Imagine you are a director who runs a small non-profit agency in a medium-sized city. You have twenty years' experience serving the most needy and poor. Your agency deals with the homeless and the working poor, people with huge needs and few resources. You offer food and clothes, help people find shelter and provide employment training. You get a little government funding but are heavily dependent on philanthropic foundations as well as direct gifts from people in the community. The agency operates in a highly volatile and uncertain environment where funding is a never-ending challenge, staff get discouraged, problems seem to be getting worse and the political environment is increasingly harsh and blameful. What does getting to maybe offer you?

Part of the challenge in being heard is to hone what you have to say and practise saying it in a way that connects both emotionally and intellectually, both affectively and cognitively. Getting better at finding allies for innovation means becoming adept at hearing feedback about how you come across when expressing your vision and commitments, to enhance your own powerfully symbolic communications. In essence, we'd want to affirm the importance of your niche, your local knowledge, and say:

- Practise expressing your vision and calling in a way that helps you attract others of like mind and commitment. Be mindful and attentive to the reactions generated by what you say, and use those reactions to form powerful alliances for change.

We would also say, be vigilant, because as Jeff Brown understood, we are all part of the system we are hoping to change. Over time we can forget that. We may be an international organization working for human rights, whose livelihood depends on the continued presence of injustice and human rights violations. To what extent are we upholding the very interaction rules that support that vicious cycle of injustice and power abuses? The point is not to get caught up in guilt and self-condemnation, but rather to be mindful of scalar invariance. As we seek to change the bigger picture, are our means and ends consistent? Or do we perpetuate the system we are trying to change by our local interactions?

- Watch for the simple rules that sustain and hold in place the existing system, and work to understand the attractors that will need to change and be confronted in the processes of social transformation. Expect that when real change starts, your own interactions as well as those of others will change. Expect this to feel risky.

In confronting risk, the social innovator or the innovating organization often feels alone. Funders and government agencies want accountability, and that often means that the innovation or initiative comes under intense scrutiny and demands for evaluation. As many not-for-profit managers have told us, "The people who fund us are demanding data on whether we've attained our goals. They want proof of effectiveness. They're demanding accountability—and we want to be accountable. We really do. But it's a lot of work, a lot of paperwork, and it costs a lot to do evaluations, and, besides, we're not researchers. We're doers. We've figured out how to do some simple evaluations of our basic programs, but what about the big-change innovations we're starting to think about? As soon as we mention some major new initiative, someone immediately says, 'How would you evaluate it?' And then we're stymied. It's pretty discouraging."

We've heard this often over the years. Evaluation, almost always scary, has become a major barrier to social innovation. Premature and skeptical demands for accountability can shut down social innovations just as they're starting to take off. At the same time, it's not viable for social innovators to just say, "Wait, wait, wait. Trust us. We'll get to evaluation later." A key to encouraging innovation is to explore and adopt less narrow and restrictive approaches to evaluation. To all those who fund social innovation, as well as to the professional evaluators they hire, we say:

• Support social innovators in getting to maybe by helping them articulate their passion and commitment. Don't prematurely force the passion and commitment of social innovators into the boxes of operational goals and logic models. Rather, stimulate and capture the early articulation of the problem as a baseline for use later, when more formal evaluative thinking becomes appropriate and helpful.

People from the world of business and the private sector might also heed this advice. The business world, appropriately, emphasizes the bottom line. Peter Drucker, the business management guru, has turned his attention to the voluntary sector in recent years. When asked about the bottom line for non-profits, he said it came down to two words: *changed lives.*

Building on Drucker, for social innovators the bottom line is changed systems that can change lives. Systems change can't be evaluated in the way narrowly targeted projects are evaluated. At this point, we want to emphasize that unlearning old ways of thinking about and doing things (sometimes part of the process of standing still, our next chapter) can be an important part of getting to maybe. Nowhere is that more the case than in opening up how we think about and approach evaluation. The traditional, narrowly focused, bottom line–oriented, goals-based model just doesn't work. Stay with us through later chapters to find out why, and also what we offer as an alternative.

We would like to end this chapter by speaking to everyone who is trying to figure out where and how they can make a difference. We each have young adult children variously engaged in social change. As professors, we encounter a variety of students interested in the implications of complexity science as they decide where and how to commit themselves. In our work we meet many others who ask us how to get started. What do we have to say to them about getting to maybe?

• Watch and listen for those who articulate a vision that you share, who are acting on a calling that inspires you. Watch for individuals from whom you can learn. Watch for groups of fellow travellers with whom you can journey. Take the plunge, prepared to learn—to be disappointed, to be energized, to be up and down, but most of all to learn—about what works for you, what engages you, what matters to you, where you feel you can make a difference. Consider your own calling. Perhaps you, too, will find yourself called to social innovation.

And, most importantly:

• Allow for imperfections—in yourself and others.

We began this book by noting that we are directing ourselves to flawed people who are not happy with the ways things are and would like to make a difference. We added that, of course, there are no people who aren't flawed. This includes both social innovators *and,* most certainly, those who would presume to advise them.

People engage in social innovation usually out of a sense of idealism, hope or urgency. Ironically, our own sense of mission may heighten our intolerance for the imperfections among those who otherwise inspire and lead us. It can also make us doubly aware of our own inadequacies and limitations. But nothing we have learned about social innovation indicates that we have to be perfect, that we cannot fail if a social innovation is to succeed. In fact, as Schoenfeld's poem at the beginning of this chapter says, "the universe gives us extra chances."

When a parent's dream for a child doesn't materialize, the parent just dreams another dream. Dandelions grow in unexpected places. There is no correlation between the "perfection" of the individual and the social innovation that results. Indeed, expecting social innovators to be perfect is another way of reinforcing the status quo.

And that's the good news from complexity science. Emergent systems thrive on interdependencies. Every person, contributing what he can, can make a difference, but no one person can claim responsibility. Moreover, what may appear at a particular moment as a defect can, from a systems perspective, attract needed energy to support unexpected realignments and new synergies, features of flow that we'll explore in Chapter 5.

This is all part of the inherent uncertainty that characterizes complex dynamics. Notice again our title: not getting to certainty, but certainly getting to maybe, to possibility. That's where social innovation begins.

Stand still. The trees ahead and bushes beside you
Are not lost. Wherever you are is called Here,
And you must treat it as a powerful stranger,
Must ask permission to know it and be known.
The forest breathes. Listen. It answers,
I have made this place around you,
If you leave it, you may come back again, saying Here.
No two trees are the same to Raven.
No two branches are the same to Wren.
If what a tree or a branch does is lost on you,
Then you are surely lost. Stand still. The forest knows
Where you are. You must let it find you.

David Wagoner, "Lost"

3. Stand Still

By now, the Grameen Bank seems like an institution rather than one of the most notable social inventions of our time. Thirty years old and with 2.5 million borrowers to its name, most of them women and all of them poor, the bank has spawned imitators around the world who offer "micro-credit" to people no regular financial institution would consider worth the risk. And yet this institution started with one man trying to understand a problem.

An economist by training, thirty-two-year-old Muhammad Yunus returned to Bangladesh in 1972, after the War of Independence. He had been studying at Vanderbilt University in the United States, and he was one of a number of expatriates who had been trying to imagine a future for their country. As he wrote in his autobiography, "We wanted to uphold democracy. We wanted to ensure the people's rights to a free and fair election and to a life devoid of poverty." He came back after independence because he knew he had to "participate in the work of nation building. I thought I owed it to myself."[1] He took the fate of his homeland personally.

He was offered a job at the government's planning commission, but he soon found it a bore and resigned to take the position of head of the Economics Department at Chittagong University. There he thought he could tackle the challenge of poverty, largely ignored by economic theory. For a couple of years, he watched the communities around him and reflected deeply on his own field and on poverty's intractability.

By 1974, Bangladesh was in the grip of a famine. It outraged Yunus that the university grounds were an oasis, while all around them the land lay barren and thousands of people starved because of lack of irrigation. "If a university is a repository of knowledge," he wrote, "then some of this knowledge should spill over to the neighboring communities. A university should not be an island where academics reach out at higher and higher levels of knowledge without sharing any of their findings."[2]

He leapt into hands-on work, unusual for an economist, experimenting with different crops and irrigation methods to help farmers grow more food. He soon realized that while farming innovations helped small landowners, their success highlighted a problem he had not focused on before: none of this directly benefited the landless poor—often women—who worked for the landowners during harvest for wages insufficient to feed themselves and their families. Yunus wanted to help them, but to do so he needed to deliberately set sail in unknown waters.

He began visiting the poorest households around him to see for himself where the challenges lay. Going to school in the 1960s in the United States, he had been inspired by the power of the civil rights movement and the young people who took to the streets to protest the war in

Vietnam. In Bangladesh, he tried to instill in his students the same belief that they could transform their communities and country. He recruited students to visit the surrounding villages to find ways to improve the lot of the poor. And one day Yunus had a seminal encounter, with the stool makers of Jobra village.

The stool makers, almost all women with children, were caught in a terrible bind. In order to make stools, they needed to buy bamboo. To buy bamboo, they needed to borrow money, but the loan had to be repaid as soon as the stool was sold. The interest charged by the middlemen was so exorbitant that the stool maker cleared barely enough to buy food for her children. So the next day she had to borrow money again to buy the bamboo, and the cycle continued. Here is Yunus's own account of one woman's life:

> Sufiya Begum earned two cents a day. That was the knowledge that shocked me. In my university courses, I theorized about sums in the millions of dollars, but here before my eyes the problems of life and death were posed in terms of pennies. Something was wrong. Why did my university courses not reflect the reality of Sufiya's life? I was angry, angry at myself, angry at my economics department and the thousands of intelligent professors who had not tried to address this problem and solve it. It seemed to me that the existing economic system made it absolutely certain that Sufiya's income would be kept perpetually at such a low level that she could never save a penny and would never invest in expanding her economic base. Her children were condemned to live a life of penury, of hand-to-mouth survival, just as she had lived it before and as her parents did before her. I had never heard of anyone suffering for the lack of twenty-two

cents. It seemed impossible to me, preposterous. Should
I reach into my pocket and hand Sufiya the pittance she
needed for capital? That would be so simple and easy.
I resisted the urge to give Sufiya the money she needed.
She was not asking for charity. And giving one person
twenty-two cents was not addressing the problem on any
permanent basis.[3]

Sufiya Begum's daily struggle to find the twenty-two cents she needed
for bamboo to make her stool was the trigger that backed Yunus against
the wall. From that moment on, he felt a compulsion to act—our
definition of a calling. His story echoes Geldof's, Brown's and
Lundström's, but Yunus was an academic who had just spent four
intense years studying the circumstances that added up to poverty in
Bangladesh. He was able to stand still and perceive the nature of the
vicious circle that kept Sufiya Begum and many like her on the edge of
starvation. And then he used that knowledge to intervene.

What if he could create a way to loan money to women such as Sufiya
Begum? This question was the starting point down a path that led him to
conclude that credit is a human right.

The loans didn't have to be big. Clearly in the case of the stool makers,
twenty-two cents a day would suffice if they didn't have to pay the
exorbitant interest rates charged by the local moneylenders. But a regular
bank would not be interested in the proposition: the amounts were too
small, the rate of return too low and people such as Sufiya Begum had
no collateral, no credit history and no guarantor who would co-sign for
the money. Then there was the fact that individual twenty-two-cent
loans would be a nightmare to track.

But Yunus didn't want to just give the money away: he saw that as substituting dependence on charity for exploitation by the middlemen, leaving the vicious cycle unbroken. His next brainstorm? Remake the local social structure to support his "bank." He would deal with small groups of borrowers, who would be issued a group loan and all of whom would reinforce the need to pay the loan back. The group itself would track the individual loans.

Yet that wasn't enough, as Yunus wrote in his autobiography: "In Jobra we discovered that it is not always easy for borrowers to organize themselves into groups. A prospective borrower first has to take the initiative and explain how the bank works to a second person. This can be particularly difficult for a village woman. She often has a difficult time convincing her friends—who are likely to be terrified, skeptical or forbidden by their husbands to deal with money—but eventually a second person, impressed by what Grameen has done for another household, will take the lead of joining the group. . . . But often, just when the group is ready, one of the five members changes her mind, saying, 'No, my husband won't agree. He doesn't want me to join the bank.' So the group falls back to four or three and sometimes even to one. And that one has to start all over again."[4]

The vicious cycle of debt repayment was amplified by a culture of poverty that defined women as worthless and incapable, and made them subservient to others and doubting of themselves. The social order kept this culture of poverty in an obdurately stable state. Yunus's challenge, and the challenge of all the people forming small groups to gain access to capital, was to change this system. This took years, not months, but one by one groups that formed tasted success—building their enterprises and reliably repaying loans.

Looking back it is possible to see the magnitude of success. From those first few groups, Grameen Bank grew to 1,175 branches, providing services in 41,000 villages, covering more than 60 percent of Bangladesh. Micro-credit initiatives that imitate Grameen Bank provide loans to an estimated 25 million more of the world's poor. While it took the determination of thousands, without Muhammad Yunus's insight and passion Grameen Bank would not exist.

Muhammad Yunus could not help being called into action. But he also spent time in analysis and reflection—and not just once. Analysis *and* passion led him to return to Bangladesh, to focus on the rural poor and their need for funding. Analysis and passion led him to adjust his model as time went on, over and over again, to keep striving for a better way.

—

Social innovators are explorers. To find their way, they have to stay tuned to the patterns around them, even as these patterns shift. Classic strategic models encourage people to think long and hard, gather all the data and then act, as if everything is logical and can be anticipated by careful planning. Parents routinely tell their impulsive children to think before they leap. But people such as Yunus can develop the ability to stand still in the middle of the action, to tease out the pattern around them in order to understand deeply the dynamic they seek to change.

David Bornstein studies how such innovators act as transformative forces, using their innovative ideas to address major problems in spite of many roadblocks.[5] He interviewed one hundred successful social innovators around the world, and found they shared a number of qualities. In particular, they trusted their intuition—their perceptions of problems—and they learned through action. In short, they were able to marry reflection and action. This is rare. We live, by and large, in a culture that divorces contemplation or reflection from action. We go to school, a time of contemplation, to prepare ourselves for action. Those who never wish to enter the world of action remain in school, as academics, or become monks, writers, artists. Those who spring into action rarely find time for contemplation, for standing still—except on vacation, when they collapse from overwork.

Deep reflection demands careful observation, not only of the details but also of their relationship to each other. "No two trees are the same to Raven / No two branches are the same to Wren," writes David Wagoner in his poem, "Lost." And he continues, "If what a tree or a branch does is lost on you / Then you are surely lost." Successful social innovators are thoughtful actors and restless thinkers. Note that Wagoner doesn't treat the tree or the branch as stationary. In relationship to the raven and the wren, the branches are doing, not just being. The need for *ongoing* reflection is shaped by the fact that in complex systems, no pattern stays in place for long and no intervention has a predictable result. The world is not acted upon, but rather interacts with us in often surprising ways. As Shakespeare's Brutus claimed, "There is a tide in the affairs of men / which, when taken at the flood, leads on to fortune." A sense of timing is key: the instinctive feeling for when to move and when to stay still. The right timing is as much given as it is created.

Sometimes challenging the accepted wisdom may seem like spitting into the wind, a dampening experience. At other times, such a challenge changes everything. Would the Grameen Bank have been possible if Muhammad Yunus had not returned to Bangladesh? More importantly, if larger events had not interceded and if the more immediate environment had not supported his efforts, would his attempts to address poverty have amounted to anything more than spitting into the wind? In our account, his success feels inevitable, but that wasn't how it seemed to him at the time. He felt lonely, and without allies:

> The 1974 famine dragged on and on, and the worse it became the more agitated I grew. Unable to stand it any longer I went to see the vice-chancellor of the university. A popular social commentator and novelist, Abul Fazal was considered by many to be the conscience of the nation. He greeted me politely.
>
> "What can I do for you, Yunus?" he asked. A ceiling fan turned slowly overhead. Mosquitoes buzzed. His orderly brought tea.
>
> "Many people are dying of starvation, yet everyone is afraid to talk about it," I responded.
>
> Abul Fazal nodded. "What do you propose?"
>
> "You are a respected man. I would ask you to make a statement to the press."
>
> "Yes, but what?"
>
> "A call to the nation and its leadership to end the famine. I am certain that all teachers on this campus will co-sign their names to your letter if you take the lead. It would help mobilize national opinion."
>
> "Yes." He sipped his tea. "Yunus," he said, "you write the statement and I will sign it."
>
> I smiled. "You are the writer. You will know what words to put in the statement."
>
> . . . The more I insisted that he was the perfect man to bring national attention to bear on the famine, the more Abul Fazal encouraged me to write the letter. He pushed his point so strongly that I had no alternative but to promise I would try. That evening I wrote out a statement. The next morning

I brought the draft to the vice-chancellor and waited while
he read it.

When he finished, Abul Fazal reached for his pen and
said, "Where do I sign?"

I was stunned. "But it is strongly worded. Maybe you want
to change some things or suggest other ideas."

"No, no, no, it is excellent," he said. And with that he
signed on the spot.[6]

This small gesture—Abul Fazal putting his signature to Yunus's own
words—was pivotal; it gave Yunus the support he needed within his own
university and, in his own words, "started a chain reaction." If he had
had a different administration, if the famine had not occurred when it
did, if he had not returned to Bangladesh . . . the list of ifs is always
endless. However, the circumstances were right and *Yunus knew it*. As
David Bornstein discovered, social innovators are experts at knowing
their markets. This is not to say that they know them perfectly, or for all
time, but in the moment they are able to grasp the pattern. They have
the courage to act on what they grasp. And their action produces a new
pattern, which they are again able to see.

How difficult is it to grasp the pattern and act on it?

Parker Palmer, American philosopher and educational activist, believes
it is quite difficult.[7] It requires not only knowledge of the world but also
self-knowledge. Palmer is widely respected for the depth of his thinking,
his devotion to teaching and teachers, and his use of poetry to help
people find meaning in their work. In his unassuming way, he has
helped thousands of people understand the connection between self-
knowledge and worldly knowledge by citing an ancient Taoist story
of a woodcarver who is required by a prince to carve a bell stand. The

woodcarver succeeds brilliantly, but when people attribute his virtuoso performance to spirits with whom he must have great connections, he suggests, most humbly, that it was a more human process. First he cleared his mind of all worldly concerns (fear of what might happen to him if he disappointed the prince, ambition, greed) by fasting for seven days. At the end of his fast, the world and even his body were forgotten. Then the woodcarver went into the forest to see the trees in their natural state:

> When the right tree appeared before my eyes,
> The bell stand also appeared in it, clearly, beyond doubt.
> All I had to do was to put forth my hand
> And begin.
> If I had not met this particular tree
> There would have been
> No bell stand at all.
> What happened?
> My own collected thought
> Encountered the hidden potential in the wood;
> From this live encounter came the work
> Which you ascribe to the spirits.[8]

This story brilliantly links innovation to a particular conversation between thought and action, and between innovator and context. Social innovators, such as Muhammad Yunus and Jeff Brown, are experts at collected thought. But notice the role of the forest, or the world and of chance relationships and live encounters. The bell stand could not have existed without the skill of the woodcarver. But, equally, it could not have existed without this particular tree and the space for the two to meet.

What is the equivalent of the "bell stand in the tree"—the pattern that is visible to the prepared mind? And why does the thing remain hidden one time when you reach out your hand, and yet another time the same gesture releases a thing of power and beauty?

—

C.S. Holling, known to his friends and colleagues as Buzz, is a man with a mission. In spite of many accolades and great respect in the academic world and from practising ecologists, he shows no signs of arrogance. Instead, he maintains a childlike curiosity and interest in how nature (both physical and social) works. He is fascinated by the patterns he sees in ecological systems and lately has come to see these same patterns in social and political systems and artistic forms. He believes that he and his multidisciplinary team of colleagues are beginning to understand one of the key properties of healthy systems—resilience.[9]

Resilience is the capacity to experience massive change and yet still maintain the integrity of the original. Resilience isn't about balancing change and stability. It isn't about reaching an equilibrium state. Rather, it is about how massive change and stability paradoxically work together.

Where do we see resilience? Since this is a book about social transformation, let's look at two levels of social transformation—the individual and the organization. As an individual, some of you reading this book will have experienced a period in your life when nothing seemed to stay the same. Everything seemed to happen simultaneously: the loss of a spouse or child; divorce; moving to a new community or even a new country; taking on a new job or suddenly being without a job; tectonic shifts that came in twos and threes, and were on you before you had time to cope. During such periods of massive change, nothing seems to be the same. And yet, you are still you. There is an integrity to you that isn't altered in spite of all of the changes in your circumstances.

Or picture an old, well-established company. After several decades of focusing on one industry, the company's leaders decide to shift their efforts into a new, emerging industry. Many employees leave the company as it goes through its transformation; the locations for the business may change too. Yet it is still recognizable as the same company. Some of its key values and functions remain intact and stable in spite of the massive reorientation.

In both of these cases, the individual and the organization were resilient. They changed and remained the same simultaneously.

This is a comforting thought in that it gives us a touchstone, something to ground us as we experience turmoil. But unless we take the time to stand still—to reflect on the pattern—resilience can be overlooked.

Holling began his work in resilience by looking at ecosystems, particularly forests. He was fascinated by how often forests that had existed for hundreds of years went through massive change. Protecting them from fires, disease or drought was no way to guarantee their continued existence. Rather, forests seemed to use these massive changes as part of their ongoing evolution.

Holling began to visualize this capacity for resilience as having four stages, which he termed release, reorganization, exploitation and conservation. The cycle of stages is continuous and simultaneous. And it is ubiquitous to healthy ecosystems, though it is fraught with challenges. Holling described the four stages as the adaptive cycle.

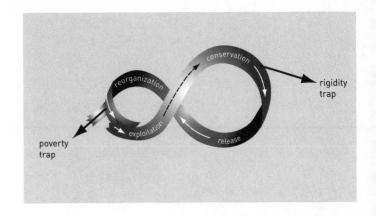

The resilience feedback loop[10]

It's a common human reaction to view a forest fire, a plague of locusts or a bank collapse as an unmitigated disaster from which nothing happy can result. But Holling argued that while disasters do destroy existing structures, they also *release* trapped resources and nutrients for new life. For instance, if all the water and nutrients in a region supported existing trees, burning down those trees released those nutrients to feed new growth.

Economist Joseph Schumpeter coined a term to describe this same idea in the 1940s: creative destruction. He noticed that healthy economies go through cycles of destruction that seemed to release innovation and creativity. The pattern Schumpeter saw in economies, Holling saw in ecosystems. In both natural and economic systems, after a phase of growth, followed by a phase in which that growth was conserved, there seemed to be the need for release. Failure to release the creativity for the next phase created a rigidity to the system, which Holling described as the "rigidity trap."

When we can see only one way to do things, we run the risk of the rigidity trap.

The Grameen Bank is an example of bringing new perspectives to a system caught in a rigidity trap. Sufiya Begum, and others like her, could see only one way to make a living: working day and night to pay back a loan and then borrowing again in an endless cycle. Yunus knew reaching into his pocket and giving her money would not break the rigidity trap, but perpetuate it. Instead, he started down the road that defined credit as a human right and focused on how to change the broader system, also caught in a rigidity trap. The banks could see no way to lend money to the poor who were bad credit risks. Yunus saw another way: creating groups to act as backup to the borrower.

Change of this kind is always difficult. It often means stopping doing something that we have done for years. It may mean leaving a job, ending a program, abandoning an approach or a system that has served us well. But the adaptive cycle tells us that unless we release the resources of time, energy, money and skill locked up in our routines and our institutions on a regular basis, it is hard to create anything new or to look at things from a different perspective. Without those new perspectives, and the continuous infusion of novelty and innovation in our lives, our organizations and our systems, there is a slow but definite loss of resilience, and an increase in rigidity.

This risk is run by even the best systems; in fact, achieving excellence in performance may make us more vulnerable to rigidity traps. Danny Miller studied companies that at one point were lauded for their excellence.[11] He discovered that in order to achieve that excellence, the companies pursued what he called an "architecture of simplicity." They focused all their resources on the one best way: they reduced slack to be lean and mean, and they reduced redundancy to ensure everyone and everything was focused on their strategic priorities. As a result, they lost peripheral vision and perspective. Like Icarus, in flying too close to the sun, they forgot that their wings were made of wax. At the moment of greatest success they found themselves knocked off course by rivals they didn't even see coming.

Miller's message, like that of Holling, is that hanging on to what we do best, when it is no longer working, is a trap. The trap makes the fall longer and harder. Social innovators like Yunus are much more comfortable than many of us at "seeing"—keeping perspective, maintaining peripheral vision. They know that for novelty to enter the world, change is necessary. And for some that change will feel like a loss of the cherished, familiar and safe.

—

The phase after release, or creative destruction, is a time of reorganization. This is when new opportunities are sought and new connections made. During this phase, there is intense competition for available space and resources. Imagine a field cleared by a forest fire. New life quickly grows. Where seeds from birch, maple and aspen trees have landed, you might see a dozen new plants crop up an inch or so apart. Overnight, seedlings cover the ground with a blanket of new life. In organizations or social groups, this reorganization phase can be a heady time of exploration; anything seems possible and the mood is optimistic.

However, ecosystems or social systems can get trapped here too. Holling and his group call this the "poverty trap," which happens when none of the new ideas seem to take root or thrive. As exciting as the reorganization phase is, with its climate of exploration and promise of renewal, if the system is to be resilient, some death is required at this stage too. Multiple species growing one inch apart cannot all grow to maturity. In an ecosystem, some species must wither while others "win," securing enough of the available resources to grow to maturity. In creative organizations, multiple teams often compete to create the best prototypes, but only a few of the programs and services that are imagined can be launched. So some of the richness, some of the variety, must be let go, allowed to die in order to move to the next phase of the adaptive cycle: exploitation.

In the exploitation stage the system invests heavily in the dominant species or winning proposal—and the species and project draws heavily on the available resources. In the social sector this means we move from the idea to the hard work of making it real; we exploit all available resources to bring the proposed idea to fruition. Social innovators rarely look back at the avenues they didn't take; the multiple possibilities for making a difference that might have flitted through the minds of Lundström, Pritchard, Brown and Yunus when they felt called to action fell away before the demands of building a new product line, buying a particular house and starting a bicycle repair operation, doing outreach in the streets and putting into place the new lending system. Social innovators, like Parker Palmer's woodcarvers, do stand still, do see the whole system, but they also immerse themselves in the reality of each stage and phase of the social innovation cycle. Analysis does not result in paralysis. They both stand still *and* act.

The last of the four adaptive stages is the conservation or maturity stage. In the forest, the trees become mature and dominate the landscape. Their dominance limits the opportunity for new growth. The large trees consume all of the resources and create shaded ground such that new life, dependent on sunlight, cannot grow. In organizations or movements, this is the "mature product or program" stage where we see return on our efforts. We have invested sufficiently in projects or services that we can now reap the benefits. But if profits blind us to the need for release, we may not recognize that this moment of success is also the time when we need to think about releasing resources for the next "back loop."

Resilience is about avoiding the traps—both of rigidity and poverty— that prevent the system from evolving. But resilience also involves taking some of who we are, what we know and what we value with us as we move between stages. Moving from stage to stage can feel like a crisis, like we are losing ourselves. But the adaptive cycle reminds us that destruction and renewal, death and life are necessary for any healthy system. The Greek root word for "crisis" means "to sift." Sifting suggests we are letting go of what is no longer necessary but retaining the essence. Resilience represents this capacity to sift: to let go and hang on simultaneously. The challenge is knowing what and how to let go.

Standing still seems particularly daunting when the forest is burning around us. And yet this is what the adaptive cycle model suggests we do. Social sector organizations run the risk of falling into the poverty trap when they are unable to focus and make choices about what to build and what to let go.

Avoiding the rigidity trap may be even harder, requiring discipline and courage. Some organizations have institutionalized the escape from the rigidity trap by putting limits on the length of projects. This forced death of a project every few years allows for a release of trapped energy, time and money. There is some arbitrariness to setting a drop-dead date for a project, but on the other hand it mitigates some of the emotional cost involved with letting go of a cherished initiative. The creativity released can either be reinvested in the organization or movement, or invested elsewhere.

Holling saw that healthy ecosystems experienced all four stages continuously and even simultaneously at different scales. The healthy forest was resilient—it used each stage as input for the next. But overly managed forests weren't resilient at all. Human caretakers planted too few species or put out fires before they had a chance to do their work—to burn out the underbrush and release nutrients in seeds, for example. These forests became brittle and vulnerable. When disaster struck—a fire that was out of control or a disease—the forest either did not go through the natural release and reorganization phases or took and extraordinarily long time—decades—to progress through phases that other forests would do in months or years. In organizations or movements, holding on to the status quo too long is similar to the overly managed forest. There is comfort in the maturity phase; we know what we are doing and how to do it. But that comfort can blind us to the need for release and reorganization, which brings renewal.

—

In the late 1980s a small group of people began meeting in Vancouver, British Columbia, to think about futures that were not their own.[12] Each had a child with a disability. Together, they considered their joys and their fears as parents. They pondered their children's dreams, their security and their place in the world. All of the parents bore scars from the political battles and guerrilla actions they had fought to win schooling, housing, medical and psychological care, and money for their children. They knew the system well and could negotiate it. But they were tired. And they were afraid.

Their struggle on behalf of their children, combined with advances in health care, meant that their children were likely to outlive them. Sooner or later, those children would be orphaned, cast into an institutional world that could not protect them from the devastating loneliness that these parents feared the most. These parents were plagued by self-doubt. Had they spent precious years fighting for resources and establishing non-profit groups that, in the end, dealt only with the needs of their children when their parents were alive? Jack Collins was there, with his daughter, Pam. Ruefully, he recognized, "We all spent years building these non-profit organizations that were supposed to be providing services to our children, but they did not really look at the needs of the person . . . Our local association for community living didn't offer anything but programs that suited the needs of the association . . . Whenever we asked for something for Pam, they put her in a training program. They trained her to bake muffins once."

Along with Collins, these parents had been intimately involved in many of these non-profit organizations, founding them, working for them, sitting on their boards, lobbying government. They knew a lot about governance and policy, legal and financial issues. They had particular expertise in estate planning; several people in the group were involved in workshops that helped parents develop wills and trusts appropriate for supporting offspring with disabilities. But the parents felt that the structures they had helped create were missing something vital.

This small group wanted to create something entirely different, an organization, a movement, a way of understanding the world that would secure the futures of their children and others like them by acknowledging and responding to their deepest human needs, not simply their handicaps.

Helped by small research and planning grants, the group spent three years in deep inquiry. Slowly, a fresh way of understanding the disabled community and the organizations meant to serve them began to emerge, and with it a small set of common and powerful themes. The group determined that four elements could add up to a good life: family and friends; financial security; a home that is a sanctuary, not a warehouse; and the ability to have one's wishes and choices respected.

In 1989, the group created a new organization called PLAN, for Planned Lifetime Advocacy Network, to realize this new approach. Al Etmanski and Vickie Cammack were part of the founding group and became the first employees of the organization: Etmanski as part-time executive director and Cammack as full-time administrator.

Etmanski exudes patience and passion. His daughter Liz and her challenges with disabilities profoundly changed his life. Eventually, his quest to improve his daughter's life and the lives of others like her became not only his avocation but also his full-time vocation. Cammack, his wife, joined him in the quest to find creative and powerful ways to improve the lives of those with disabilities and their families.

As founders of PLAN, they wanted to transcend ideas of simple care in order to tease out the elements of creating a good life for their children. Their challenge was how to achieve these goals.

They realized that all of the elements—a home, family and friends, choice, even security—involved the cultivation of meaningful personal relationships. Relationships did not *lead to* quality of life; they *were* quality of life. As their understanding of this principle grew and became subtler, members also recognized that the safety they sought for their sons and daughters could not be separated from this quality of life. They discovered research that had already been done on a proper safety net for people with disabilities. As Ted Kuntz, a board member of PLAN, later wrote: "The results of the research demonstrated that the safety of people with a disability was not dependent upon the number of social workers, law enforcement officers, by-laws, or other methods of enforcement . . . Rather, their safety was dependent upon the number of relationships the person had. The more relationships, the greater their safety. The fewer relationships, the greater their vulnerability."[13]

The necessary relationship was not a professional one. It had to be like the relationship between a parent and a child, or between friends: a loving relationship, a relationship of encounter and attention, a relationship integrated into the full life of each person and built upon mutual giving and mutual being. It was not a one-way street, with the person with a disability at the receiving end.

Looking back on this period, Etmanski describes it as follows: "We had to fight for these concepts. They didn't just slip into your hand and you'd say, 'Oh, I think I'll follow that one for a while.' We would go over an issue five meetings in a row, agree on something, and then at the sixth meeting decide to go in a completely different direction. We were civil, but there was tension there to figure out what the values meant . . . There was a lot of comfort in ambiguity . . . I had come from a job in which I made twenty decisions a day—probably all of them were bad decisions, but I was able to make them—to a job in which I was expected to make no decisions for months. We persevered, walked around the issue, had a look at it, said, 'Okay, this is it; we might as well go in this direction.' And then we'd change our minds . . . We were a learning group. Everyone was curious."

Like so many innovations, PLAN began in 1989 with a sense that something had to be done. The system had failed them, but out of this failure the families took heart, not despair. There had to be a better way. If release or "creative destruction" can be said to be a psychosocial space, the PLAN parents were in it. Parents were giving up or letting go of one dream, of one way of doing things, and searching for another. A sense of sadness or even despair was coupled with a deep sense of conviction that some different way was possible. This hope sustained people through a period in which direction was unclear and there was little to go on, other than the energy of other people willing to join in.

As others joined in, however, the innovation moved into reorganization and exploration mode. This phase in PLAN's case is beautifully described by Etmanski, as a time characterized by "deep inquiry, immersed in profoundly honest, occasionally contentious dialogue with each other and with the world around them." While the exact moment of transition is not clear, at last all the conversation began to converge on the notion of relationships. And then it was time to give the ideas a tangible form.

In 1989, with one full-time administrator, a half-time executive director, a tiny office in Vancouver and still only the vaguest idea of what it would all mean eventually, PLAN was born. Its founders could hold onto only their hard-won, intuitive first principle: "Relationships did not *lead to* quality of life; they *were* quality of life." All the details of execution remained to be clarified.

Haunted by the compromises and co-optation they had seen in other organizations, the founders decided that independence was key, no matter how vulnerable it left them financially. They resolved to accept no government funding. Instead, each member family would enter into a lifetime relationship with PLAN, and contribute an initial membership fee (currently $1,500) and $350 annual dues. Families would also help underwrite the direct services they used by paying an hourly fee. While the organization would solicit private and corporate donations to cover shortfalls, they never wanted to be beholden to large funders or imprisoned by their own organizational needs. To safeguard PLAN's independence and authenticity, the founders also decided that a majority of the board of directors would always be representatives of member families.

—

PLAN's goal was to find ways to extend the children's human networks, but how do you grow a set of relationships? To begin, the parents decided, each "child" member would be the person at the centre. Then PLAN would hire a part-time consultant or facilitator to get to know the person, to look for existing relationships and coach them into full flower, and to create new relationships wherever possible. The facilitator would be more an explorer than an engineer, and each network was to be unique, composed of an unpredictable array of immediate family members, distant relatives, old friends, new volunteers, co-workers and neighbours. Where a relationship already existed for the person at the centre, the facilitator and other network members would work to enrich it, to help it move from the accidental and occasional to the purposeful and rhythmic. When the relationship involved a fresh volunteer, the facilitator would face the trickier task of introducing two people into each other's worlds. In either case, as things progressed and network members became engaged, the facilitator's role would fade into the background, usually resolving into nothing more than an occasional check-in or get-together.

The networks took time to build. Often it was a few years before they were deep enough and robust enough to be sustainable. But as time passed, PLAN was able to point to many vibrant, long-term networks, and its reputation grew.

There were surprises along the way. Once a network became sustainable, support and advocacy flowered from it naturally, and isolation and alienation faded away, at least as much as they ever truly fade for any of us. Members talked about their networks as extended families. People who had not known each other previously become intimate friends, drawn together by their love for and commitment to the person at the centre. Families began to rely on the networks, too, even assigning decision-making rights to key network members when the families were out of town or unreachable.

PLAN members began to discover that giving was truly a two-way street.

Al Etmanski tells the story of Emily, a young woman in her twenties with multiple disabilities as a result of a head injury received in a car accident when she was two years old. Since that time she had lived in a hospital. She was unable to walk, talk or feed herself, and she had had no contact with her family for many years. Feeding her was a time-consuming task, and when PLAN first came into her life, the hospital had planned to have all of her teeth removed to make feeding easier for the nurses. PLAN began to develop a network of friends around Emily, and they were able to prevent the removal of her teeth. As her relationships deepened, the friendship and human contact seem to bring her to life. After a short time, Emily was able to leave the hospital and move to a group home.

One of the members of Emily's network was Ann, an extremely active grandmother. Ann was always working on one community project or another, serving on multiple committees, and contributing to the world in a variety of ways. Ann got into the habit of preparing an elegant dinner for Emily once a week, packing it up with her best plates and silverware, and spending two or three hours sitting with Emily and feeding her. When Ann was asked what she felt Emily got out of their weekly meetings, she said that it was easy to see: Emily loved the company and loved the food, and even though she couldn't say anything, her delight and involvement were written on her face. When Ann was asked what value she received from her time with Emily, she smiled, and then said that it was the only part of her week in which she wasn't rushing around. Emily's gift of time allowed Ann to slow down and to connect to another human being in a meaningful and profoundly peaceful way.

PLAN was slowly growing its networks—by the mid-1990s, it had fostered fifty of them. Meanwhile, Al Etmanski, with help from Jack Collins and Vickie Cammack, was capturing the innovation on paper. He started by trying to write a useful, technical handbook on financial planning, but it evolved into an evocative summary of years' worth of reflection, dialogue and practice. In 1996 the board made the decision to underwrite its publication.

The book was called *Safe and Secure,* and it helped PLAN win a B.C. Broadcasters Award. In the 1980s the major media outlets in British Columbia had decided to pool their philanthropic resources. Rather than offering small donations—a public service announcement here, a sponsorship there—to hundreds of different organizations, they selected one organization a year to support. The award was worth roughly three million dollars in free airtime and print space. With the award, PLAN was able to sell more books and develop numerous relationships: London Drugs agreed to distribute *Safe and Secure* through its outlets; B.C. Hydro brought PLAN in as a supplier to its Employee Assistance Program to help employees with children with disabilities cope and plan for the future; Vancity Credit Union entered into a three-year agreement to work with PLAN. Law firms began to pay more attention to PLAN's approach to trust and estate planning. The Insurance Corporation of British Columbia became interested in PLAN, and that interest ultimately led to a separate ICBC edition of the book that focused on assisting individuals with head injuries as a result of vehicular accidents.

By 1999, PLAN was an established success with an increasing national profile. Demands poured in from other regions of the country for help with starting replica projects. Each new start-up organization had legal autonomy, but PLAN played an intensive organizing, training and consulting role. Within four years there were roughly a dozen affiliates across Canada.

And as PLAN worked to start other organizations, its own organization was also growing. By 2003 it had 116 networks, and was wondering whether it needed to set limits to keep its core operation from growing too large. Also, government officials were beginning to take the organization quite seriously, and PLAN began to have an effect on provincial policy. First, in response to the group's advocacy, the province raised the asset limit for those receiving disability benefits. This was a technical change, but it had a dramatic impact on families working to establish financial security for their children with disabilities. A lawyer who is one of PLAN's oldest and most ardent supporters admits to being baffled by PLAN's ability to work the legislative machinery on such a technical and contentious issue. He shrugs his shoulders and says simply, "It was a magic trick pulled off by Al." Others in the organization believe that they are able to engage policy makers in such a way that they can see and feel the human consequences of various decisions.

A much more dramatic and potentially farther-reaching example involved the definition of legal competence and capacity in British Columbia.

PLAN has always worked to ensure that its members with disabilities are allowed to participate in the decisions, big and small, that affect their lives. In the 1990s the organization led a massive law reform effort to change guardianship legislation so that the courts would recognize the ability to form and sustain meaningful relationships as one factor in determining a person's capacity to appoint others to assist with decision making. PLAN argued that relationship or "interpersonal" knowledge is a powerful form of intelligence, and that those who are capable of relationships are also capable of helping to decide who their legal guardian should be (as opposed to simply having the guardian appointed by some third party). British Columbia is now the only jurisdiction in the world that includes having a "caring relationship of trust" as a factor in determining competency.

In short, PLAN leveraged its early experiences and insights to grow in size, scope and impact. By the end of the 1990s, it was a success on most fronts, with much pressure on it to replicate and grow. It had already reached the maturity or conservation stage.

In the world of social innovation, "conservation" is an ambivalent phase and phrase. On the one hand it feels like success. PLAN's radical new approach is now widely recognized. So is Jeff Brown's TenPoint Coalition. The Grameen Bank has broken all the rules, yet exceeded all expectations.

But social problems, unlike technological ones, are never entirely *solved*. Just when social innovators realize they are a success, they more than ever need to stand still in order to look for what has been left out, what counter-truths need to be addressed. It can be a bittersweet experience. Etmanski and Cammack saw that, and we'll explore how they responded when we get to "Cold Heaven." But for now, let us reflect on what they, Yunus, Holling and others teach us about *how* to stand still.

How to Stand Still

To stand still is to take stock. Perhaps for a minute, perhaps over months, social innovators ask themselves, "Am I on the right track? I believe in what we're doing, but is my faith warranted?" Where can social innovators and those who support them find answers?

As a philanthropist supporting social innovation, you might logically turn to evaluation. Isn't that what evaluation is all about—collecting data to allow people to assess how they are doing, what they have achieved? In the meetings that preceded the writing of this book, we reviewed examples of major social innovation and inevitably someone would wonder: does evaluation help or impede social innovation?

Innovation flows from creative juices. Evaluation, because of its typically critical and judgmental stance, may well inhibit creativity. Indeed, creativity and critical analysis are often juxtaposed as opposite ways of thinking. Much of the energy for social innovation flows from faith, hope and a sense of calling. Is there any place for hard-headed evaluation? Or should it be exiled, as in brainstorming exercises?

Many forms of evaluation are the enemy of social innovation if applied at the wrong time or in the wrong way. But serious social innovators want to make a difference, and need some way of determining whether what they are doing is actually working. The right kind of evaluation can be a powerful tool to help the social innovator stand still and take stock.

In the current climate of exposures of malpractice in corporate executive suites and government departments, evaluation has come to be defined rather rigidly. Funders of all kinds demand accountability and praise evidence-based practice. Many social innovators are understandably wary of such evaluation. They recognize intuitively that the early phases of social innovation in particular are not well served by traditional evaluation methods.

We want to offer a way of asking the right evaluation questions at the right time and asking them in a way that energizes rather than stifles social innovation. Such a creative approach to evaluation does exist. It is called developmental evaluation.

Developmental evaluation integrates creativity and critical thinking. It involves long-term, partnering relationships between evaluators and those engaged in innovative initiatives and development. Developmental evaluators ask probing questions and track results to provide feedback and support adaptations along the emergent path. This can be especially important in the explorative, reorganization phase of social innovation that looks and feels chaotic and is characterized by many false starts, dead ends and trial-and-error experimentation. Only when the ideas have crystallized can a more orderly, more predictable exploitation phase begin, one that takes invention and turns it into innovation. But if the ideas are not allowed to gestate in the reorganization phase, nothing really innovative can be born. Developmental evaluation is needed to nurture exploration.

Most conventional evaluators insist that an effort cannot be judged without clear, measurable goals. They spout the wisdom of the Cheshire Cat: if you don't know where you're going, any road will get you there. A road map specifying where you're going and how you'll know when you get there is essential, evaluators insist, for effective action and accountability. They are especially critical of grand schemes that vaguely envision systems change and transformation. But social innovators in complex systems learn to eschew clear, specific and measurable goals because clarity, specificity and measurability are limiting and can lead to tunnel vision. In contrast, when astute social innovators tackle an issue or a problem, they realize that they don't yet know enough to set specific goals or measurable targets; they also understand that different participants have different aims in the change process—and that those participants themselves should play a major role in goal setting. In both PLAN and the Grameen Bank, leaders immersed themselves in the community, became one with the community, and together with the community faced clear, hard realities in the context of a huge, shared vision.

Developmental evaluation offers a process for periodic reflection—systematically looking back and seriously looking ahead—to gauge progress, harvest important lessons and rigorously examine what's working and what's not. Developmental evaluation supports standing still as a foundation for the next move forward.

—

If asked by the leadership of a philanthropic foundation about the implications of standing still, we'd begin with this suggestion:

• Support those who question and inquire, not just those who have answers. Look for organizations, places and times where standing still is honoured and savoured. Support those who try to act in the context of the long view. Pay attention to the questions being asked, not just the outcomes promised, when you make funding decisions.

The funding community favours proposals that promise impressive results. But such promised results derive from assumptions, fundamental premises, and some assessment of how the world works and how to change it. Acknowledging assumptions leads to questions, not just answers. Impressive promises of results should be matched by equally impressive questions, which reveal the capacity to engage in inquiry as a part of action. Those seeking funds often are required to pretend to know more than it is possible to know, especially in highly dynamic and emergent situations. Asking different, better and more appropriate questions can eventually lead to more sophisticated answers. Thus, we'd suggest, an additional criterion for funding might be the quality of the questions that will be explored during a social innovation.

In one conversation we had with a funder, she responded: "Okay, I can see how we could encourage more authentic questioning in grant proposals, but that feels like a change in emphasis. Isn't there something more proactive we can do?"

There is, indeed. One barrier to finding new ways of seeing things is the habit of keeping arenas of action separate: health, education, environment, criminal justice and so on. We've seen first-hand the value of bringing together thoughtful and engaged social innovators from highly diverse sectors, who learn from and challenge each other. Practitioners in different fields seldom get an opportunity to listen to each other. It's important to support such reflective opportunities, even when the bang for the buck is not obvious.

This advice can also be relevant to the public sector, where bureaucratic barriers often keep ministries, departments, agencies and different levels of government from exchanging information and learning together. This is not as simple as merely convening people from different areas of responsibility. Learning to think like a movement involves paying attention to what actually joins action and theory, and cultivating skill at managing the relationship between the two. Tools like system or logic maps and other visual language can help groups and individuals see these connections, but, ultimately, encouraging individuals from different disciplines to actively listen and understand is irreplaceable. Yunus listened when he cracked the problem of the stool makers of Jobra, but it was active listening that treated the stool makers' story as a piece in a much larger puzzle of inequity and spiralling debt. This kind of standing still takes practice. Thus, we would encourage the philanthropist to work with public- and private-sector leadership to:

- Support training in systems thinking and complexity science for leaders across government departments, non-governmental agency sectors, academia and business arenas.
- Support interdisciplinary, cross-government, cross-sector think-tank groups where serious inquiries can be undertaken from a complexity perspective.

You can almost see the senior government official frowning, rolling her eyes and saying, "Study, study, study. Fine, I'm all for studying and understanding. But our constituents expect us to make decisions and take action. In the face of crisis, we can't just endlessly report that the situation is complex and we're studying what to do. *We have to act!*"

Such a moment is probably not a good time to reiterate our assertion that thinking is a form of action. In the face of a rapidly changing world, especially in times of crisis, governments are prone to two kinds of errors: (1) acting precipitously without fully understanding the situation, and (2) delaying needed action by seemingly endless studies and debate. The precipitous and rushed invasion of Iraq provides many lessons in this regard. On the other hand, it is often politically unwise or even unacceptable to delay action through endless study and debate. This chapter has emphasized the parallel and mutually reinforcing tracks of action and reflection. In the public sector, action can take the form of revisiting, reaffirming and deepening understanding of basic principles and values in the context of a new situation or crisis. At the same time, inquiry into the emergent nature of the situation is needed. The hoped-for result is to stay appropriately policy focused while avoiding narrow knee-jerk solutions that will quickly become irrelevant, even harmful, in the face of a rapidly changing world. We will have a great deal more to say about how to do this as the book unfolds, but at this point we would add the following to our advice to public-sector leaders:

• Support developmental evaluation as a form of reflective practice that involves ongoing data collection and assessment to help policy makers adapt their decisions and implement their principles in the face of changed conditions.

—

Voluntary-sector organizations face similar challenges but on a different scale. Part of the problem for the executive running a small non-profit in a medium-sized city is that she and her staff have no time for reflection and analysis. Tell the agency director to stand still and she looks at you with disbelief. "Stand still? There are the homeless to house, the hungry to feed, the sick to heal—how can we possibly stand still? Our proposal for continued funding is due next month. It's all we can do to stay alive in the face of declining resources and increasing demand for our services. *Stand still?* Not until they carry me out in the pine box, then I'll be lying still. But *stand still?* No way. Can't happen." Or words to that effect.

Yes, voluntary-sector organizations manage to undertake some periodic strategic-planning exercises, often under duress and because donors expect to see such exercises. These are seldom really thoughtful processes, including examining fundamental assumptions and studying data about real effectiveness. Voluntary-sector organizations fall into patterns of practice that take on the status of received wisdom: this is how we do things. In contrast, the standing-still metaphor in this chapter places a premium on recognizing both old and new patterns, including identifying and understanding the reinforcing feedback loops that hold patterns in place and system leverage mechanisms that are entry points for change. Because voluntary-sector staff typically have direct experience with what's happening in the trenches and on the front lines of programming, voluntary-sector organizations are in a unique position to engage in ongoing and emergent pattern recognition and interpretation.

But this doesn't happen naturally or easily.

These organizations need to create opportunities and incentives for staff to engage in reflective practice and connect the results with strategic thinking and decision making. We would say to the director of a small agency or voluntary-sector organization:

- Recognize that all successful innovation is a cycle and that all phases are necessary to move an idea through development to initiative to successful program.

Moreover, resilient innovations, like resilient people, need support in every phase. We need to nurture radical ideas, weed out those that will never fly, nourish the others as they gain strength, support their growth and celebrate their maturity. Recognizing the characteristics of each phase adds to the potential for successful innovation.

—

Lastly, to those who are committed to making a difference, the very people at whom we have most directly aimed this book, we would say:

- Make reflective practice a centrepiece of your action and build your skills in this area.

Practitioners tend to be action oriented, which is why they're practitioners and not academics. As a result, they may have little tolerance for engaging in reflection and analysis. The very notion of reflection can sound like a luxury, or a waste of time, or something you do after retirement from a life of action. We hope that the examples in this chapter illustrate the value of reflection and pattern recognition as skills that can enhance effectiveness and open up new opportunities for engagement.

Like any skill, reflective practice requires training and practice if it is to be well done. The process sounds simple but, in our experience, the challenges are substantial: learning pattern recognition and analysis, understanding system dynamics and complexities, and testing the underlying assumptions of long-established practice. We've seen practitioners become discouraged when what sounded like a friendly session of peers sitting around and sharing positions and practices turned into deep questioning and uncomfortable peeling back of the onion of practice. Initial sessions may yield more questions than answers and create uncertainty where previously there had been the comfort of unquestioned certainty. But those who persist and become skilled can take their practice to another, more intentional and sophisticated level.

Many who engage in social innovation take pride in impatience, as well they should. There is much to be done, much that should be done, much that must be done. Or as Woody Allen has pointed out: "Life is

full of misery, loneliness and suffering—and it's all over much too soon."
He has also noted the importance of this moment: "More than any other
time in history, mankind faces a crossroads. One path leads to despair
and utter hopelessness. The other, to total extinction. Let us pray we
have the wisdom to choose correctly."

Getting to Maybe posits a third alternative: making a better world
through social innovation. Cynicism is the easy out. On the other hand,
sincerity and vision are insufficient. In the previous chapter we
emphasized the importance of hope and calling for getting to maybe.
This chapter has emphasized coupling vision and commitment with
analysis and reflection. This coupling is a habit to cultivate early in life.

Western school systems are fundamentally grounded in simple linear
constructions of the world regardless of discipline. History courses focus
on great men (and occasionally women) and seminal events. Social
sciences look for primary causes expressed in linear predictive equations
(regression analysis). Natural sciences remain focused on the world of
predictable Newtonian physics. Traditional Western education, then,
does not school young people in complexity science or provide them with
the capacity to analyze complex systems.

We urge those who want to make a difference to begin the reflective
process by examining critically the thinking and analytic tools they've been
given. Do you know how to see the world through the lens of complexity
science? What are your pattern recognition skills? To what extent can you
trace historical developments (e.g., through the phases of the adaptive
cycle) to understand the present stage in which social innovation might be
catalyzed? These questions lead us to offer the counsel we've shared with
our own children in both words and (we hope) by example.

- Develop your capacity to see and understand complex systems, and learn to draw action implications from what you see and understand.
- Cultivate the discipline of reflective practice. Learn to value standing still long enough to see what is around you, to understand the flow of events and the context of the moment.
- As you act, evaluate the consequences of your actions and make adjustments accordingly. Don't expect to get it right the first or second or third or fourth time. Indeed, keep questioning what it even means to get it right.
- Learn to live the paradox of action as reflection, and reflection as action.

Rush hour and the urban outflow pours
across the Million Dollar Bridge. I wait
for the walk-light, cross-traffic slight but
caution's the rule when the city roars
toward all its separate homes. I get
the sign, little electric man, and step
into the street. A woman turns into
my lane, bearing down, eye-contact,
and still she guns it until I stare and
shake my head in disbelief at her
ferocity. She slows begrudged to let
me pass, runs down the window of her Saab
and shouts, "Why don't you wait for the light?"
and flips me the bird. I feel weepy like
a punished child, mind sinking to lament,
What's wrong with the human race? Too many
of us, too crowded, too greedy for space—
we're doomed, of course, so I head for coffee
and a muffin, walking sad and slow on
the return. I'm waiting again to cross,
picking fingersful of muffin from the
paper sack and watching the phalanx of
cars race by, not even a cell of a
thought in my mind that I might jump the change,
when a man who's got the green stops,
an executive wearing a crisp white
shirt and shiny red tie, and he raises
his palm to gesture me safely across,
making all the cars behind him wait while
I walk, and together at rush hour that
man and I redeem the whole human race.

Alison Hawthorne Deming, "Urban Law"

4. The Powerful Strangers

Many of us who have reflected on the need for change in the world feel powerless to do anything about it. We can see what needs to be done; indeed, there are times when injustice enrages us. But then, when it comes to acting, we face a great inner, and sometimes outer, resistance. We wonder how to start. We are crushed by early obstacles. Like the poet Alison Deming, we feel defeated when we try to step into traffic, like a punished child who doesn't know the rules, made to feel small by those who have the right of way.

In the last chapter, we used David Wagoner's poem to focus on the need to combine deep reflection and awareness of patterns with action. But according to Wagoner, after standing still, the first order of business when lost is to treat the moment as "a powerful stranger" and to develop a relationship with that stranger, to "know it and be known." This can be frightening—as frightening as being lost in the wilderness. But it can also be empowering. When Deming has her second encounter with a stranger, it is a very different kind of communication, one that "redeem[s] the whole human race." Both Wagoner and Deming agree that the powerful stranger can make or break your day. And both suggest that understanding your relationship to the power the stranger seems to possess is key to finding your way out of a forest, or across a rushing street.

So who are these enemies? In part, the powerful stranger that resists change is within us. As Pogo, the comic-strip character from the 1960s, said, "We have met the enemy and he is us." To create change we must find and confront our biases, blindness, fear and our own power, both to create and to destroy. Jeff Brown had to let go of his safe life; Linda Lundström had to let go of her belief that she was just a fashion designer who could do nothing about racial injustice. They both had to confront their prejudices against those others they eventually came to help.

And for others, who start not from safety but from rage, rebellion and a deep sense of injustice, the need is often to find forgiveness, for others and for ourselves. Bob Geldof began his autobiography with this verse from a poem by W.B. Yeats:

> Out of Ireland have we come.
> Great hatred, little room,
> Maimed me from the start.
> I carried from my mother's womb
> A fanatic's heart.[1]

Geldof identified with the Yeats poem because he spent much of his life feeling angry and resentful of those in power. But in order to create the change that would be Live Aid, he had to work with the powerful. He had to approach them on their ground, identifying with them as well as confronting them.

Power means both the power to maintain the status quo and the power to change. Power has to do with control of resources—of time, energy, money, talent and social connections. The creation of something new needs such resources. As a mature stand of trees in the forest absorbs all the light and depletes the soil of nutrients for its own purposes (making new growth on the forest floor difficult), so the established organizations and institutions in any society absorb most of the resources, sometimes leaving little for innovation. Just as a seed needs soil and light to grow into a tree, if an innovation is to transform from an idea to a reality, it needs to draw on human resources. Innovation is fuelled first by the energy, time and skills of people, but also needs financial capital and, ultimately, enough authority to penetrate the established structures so that, as Al Etmanski put it so well, the transformation becomes established in its own right, "part of the air we breathe."

But the challenge of finding resources is not only one of scarcity. In many cases social innovators meet active resistance. The history of humankind has been one of a struggle on the part of individuals and groups to amass wealth and power. In almost no societies are such things evenly distributed. Those who have wealth wish to hang onto it.[2] The divide between the powerful and the weak can be hard to bridge. In Leonard Cohen's immortal words:

> Everybody knows that the dice are loaded
> Everybody rolls with their fingers crossed
> Everybody knows that the war is over
> Everybody knows the good guys lost
> Everybody knows the fight was fixed
> The poor stay poor, the rich get rich
> That's how it goes
> Everybody knows.[3]

For the social innovator, mobilizing the power and resources to change things presents a paradox. Anyone who wishes to transform a system has to unlock resources claimed by the status quo. But the image of unlocking suggests someone standing outside the locked door—outside the system. And, as we have repeated many times, complexity theory leads us to recognize that we are part of the system we are trying to change. This is why Wagoner wrote that encountering the powerful stranger means to know and to be known.

So how do we begin? Not with certainty, and not without risk. Taking on power can be a dangerous business.

—

When HIV/AIDS first appeared in North America in the early 1980s, it was greeted with fear and confusion. It was labelled as a gay disease early, and competing definitions abounded . . . was this punishment for sin, a suite of different ailments, a curable condition or a fatal one? Confused doctors "shed" patients they were afraid of or unable to treat. Individual sufferers were isolated and shunned. But not for long.

Frustrated and frightened, the gay community began to mobilize.[4] The first HIV/AIDS sufferers confronted a formidable hierarchy. Doctors, insurers and pharmaceutical companies were the professionals who held the keys; the patients were supposed to do just that—be patient.

Perhaps conditioned by their previous struggles, gay activists first linked together to form a community of sufferers. Leaders stressed that they were neither "patients" nor "victims," but "people living with AIDS." Shedding the "patient" identity, their numbers and their anger grew, and they began to protest more actively. They attacked the doctors' right to control access to experimental drugs, the pharmaceutical companies' right to make a profit, the insurance industry's right to restrict coverage to established protocols. Soon the community became a movement, and the protest grew angrier and louder. Groups such as Wake Up Canada and AIDS Action Now! engaged in confrontation, regularly targeting pharmaceutical companies for protests at international conferences on HIV/AIDS.

Acrimony and conflict grew, but there was no accommodating response on the part of the establishment. Medical authorities, insurance companies and pharmaceutical companies closed ranks against the assault. The movement now faced a test. Non-violent conflict was not enough. It became obvious that to unlock the resources people with AIDS needed, other kinds of leaders were required, those with connections to people inside the establishment. The movement turned to doctors and lawyers within the HIV/AIDS community: people with professional skills. Confrontation with the powerful stranger gave way to bridge building and even identification.

That the movement succeeded in transferring leadership is one of the more recent stories of successful social transformation. The transfer required another, risky, change in identity, from activist to advocate. The new HIV/AIDS advocates were able to build relationships with researchers and marketers within the pharmaceutical companies and within the medical profession. But of course, in doing so, they distanced themselves from the activists whose angry protests had opened the door. The advocates walked through the doors that had been opened by the activists. But theirs was a decidedly different approach. As one pharmaceutical representative reflected, "I can remember meeting my first two head-honcho activists . . . I didn't know want to expect. I was told that the one guy that I was to meet would give me a rough time.

I found the guy to be an absolutely unbelievable gentleman—very bright, gold-medal winner . . . and with an MBA. The other guy was a business major, and we all sat down and talked about things and they asked me some pretty pointed business questions and then I gave them reasonable answers and I think that was that."[5]

The story has shades of Jeff Brown and his encounter with the street youth. In the enemy, surprisingly, we discover ourselves, sometimes a lost part of ourselves. In the HIV/AIDS story, "Advocates constructed themselves as business-minded community people while company representatives constructed themselves as community-minded business people."[6]

Despite what the pharmaceutical company representative said, this was far from easy. It required the breaking down of old boundaries and relationships and the creation of new ones. For those who used their identities as professionals to link with the medical establishment, there was a simultaneous distancing from their compatriots, other people with HIV/AIDS for whom participation in the movement was based on their shared illness. This could have resulted in accusations of co-optation, but for the most part it did not. Instead, a shift in resources occurred, allowing the old lines to be redrawn and new forms of social action to become possible.

Ultimately, through conflict and then collaboration, the North American HIV/AIDS activists/advocates were able not only to encounter the powerful strangers but also to know them and be known. They first confronted their own fears, then built links between people living with AIDS, and they were able to mobilize a new generation of leaders to connect to the powerful pharmaceutical companies and government officials who were the gatekeepers of medical resources. More drugs were covered earlier by insurance plans. Patients got access to clinical trials that abandoned the idea of a control group receiving placebos. The result was social transformation, not only around the organization of the treatment of AIDS, but also in the shift of many pharmaceutical representatives from a marketing role to an educational role, and a challenge to accepted research protocols.

But happy endings are only stations on a road or (as C.S. Holling would suggest) on an infinite loop. Some fear the new order may take on the properties of the old. Will the new AIDS elite, an alliance of the successful, professional advocates and the community-minded pharmaceutical reps, become as exclusive as the old medical bastion?[7] Will they be open to the concerns of women, intravenous drug users, immigrants? It is the nature of power in complex systems to have a "sticky" quality, certain hubs of influence taking on more and more resources and leaving the rest with much less. As Holling's four-phase model taught us, the stage after maturity and conservation is a new round of release and reorganization. We come back to where we started: "we have met the enemy and he is us" becomes "we have met the enemy and he has become us."

The story of the HIV/AIDS movement is something of a parable about the risks and rewards of engaging the powerful stranger. Early power and resources for change are often found through *connection*, through joining together with fellow travellers, like-minded individuals whose chief resources are their passion, their time and their energy. If successful at this stage, the community becomes a movement, which opens the door for *confrontation* and possibly conflict as those who control larger portions of money, authority and access resist demands for change. If the system is to be transformed as opposed to overturned, *collaboration* between the radicals and the establishment must be created. If it succeeds, deep shifts in the distribution of resources may occur. Connection, confrontation and collaboration each offer their challenges and have lessons for social innovators.

—

For those who love wild animals, this has not been a good century. Species continue to become extinct at an alarming and unprecedented rate. For many of us who live in cities, this problem may not have the same urgency as dealing with the homeless on our streets or the poor in our slums. However, for the men and women around the world engaged in trying to conserve species, the sense of despair and loss when the last member of a species dies is real and very personal. "On one occasion, I was taken out of school by my father to see the last pure-bred Norfolk Horn ram before he died," one conservationist remembers. "The next morning the breed was extinct. The sense of loss was very tangible."[8]

For the twenty years or so before his death in 2003, one of the leaders of the species conservation movement in the United States, and perhaps the world, was Ulysses S. Seal.[9] An imposing man, Seal had flowing white hair, a white beard, piercing eyes and a booming voice. Born in Virginia, Seal grew up with a love of the outdoors and of animals of all kinds. At college he studied psychology and then biochemistry, and eventually he moved to Minnesota to take a position as a biochemist, specializing in human cancers. But Seal never forgot his love of animals. As a sideline to his day job he would help out at the local zoo, taking blood samples and anaesthetizing large mammals. His greatest love was tigers.

Seal was no stranger to the dynamics of power. Or to standing still. He saw that species were becoming extinct and some animals were becoming a scarce resource for zoos who wanted to breed and exhibit them. These animals were also a scarce resource for the governments of developing countries, who saw them as tourist attractions or sources of biodiversity. They were a scarce resource for the scientists who wanted to study them, for the animal lovers and NGOs who wanted to rescue them and for the local hunters who wanted to shoot them. Each of these groups had strong feelings about how a species should be managed. They were as likely to fight as to collaborate, as humans are wont to do over scarce resources.

"For zoo directors and curators, animals were tokens to be distributed and exchanged. In earlier decades, acquiring the animals was a very small part of the overall budget of the zoo. But as species become more rare and international regulations tighter, zoo collections grew to have enormous value," Seal reflected. "Then there were the scientists. Field ecologists were deeply resentful of the people in charge of the captive community. Even if an endangered species was breeding better in captivity than in the wild, field ecologists simply insisted that all funding should go into preserving the species in the wild."

As a scientist who put a great value on data, Seal noticed that the arguments between these interested parties were informed less by knowledge than by belief and emotion. Zoos were intent on breeding endangered species but kept very few medical or life-history records about individual animals. This was a problem. Inbreeding was a major cause of species extinction in small populations, but without medical and life-history records it was very difficult to tell what was at risk with any breeding pair, particularly as animals were swapped between zoos with no records attached.

Similarly, government agencies and NGOs might become alarmed by what they saw as declining numbers of gibbons in Thailand, for instance, without any real understanding of why the species was declining or how many individuals were left. Too often, disagreements between the factions were settled not by reason but rather by who had the power or the money. The conflict was intense and at times involved players around the globe.

"Take, for example, the Arabian oryx," Seal explained. "There was an enormous amount of conflict around this animal, which is kept in over a hundred zoos in multiple countries, all with their own agendas and players. Genetic information about the animal was not shared. So there was conflict at the scientific level, conflict between continents and conflict among private entrepreneurial groups who simply purchased the animals for zoos because they are increasingly scarce."

Seal believed that there was a way to make the conservation community more effective at saving these scarce resources. Getting to maybe in this case demanded that concerned scientists and practitioners build better, science-based analyses of the status of the species and of the history of individual animals. "We don't know what's going on on the ground," said Seal, "and we don't know what's out there."

In order to create these improved analyses, Seal needed all the different organizations, each of which had a piece of the puzzle, to come to the table and share their knowledge. And, as this was difficult due to a history of conflict and mistrust, he set out to help them put aside their differences and work together. Here again, power was an issue. The scientists were seen as the elite in terms of research, but they were often intensely reluctant to share their knowledge because they felt it was incomplete or unpublished. Government agencies had legal power, and NGOs, particularly those led by Westerners, had access to the media and therefore the power of public opinion. But it was the wildlife managers in the field who ultimately were in the best position to manage the species. They were the least powerful group. As Seal said, "The key people are the managers. The scientists and specialists are there to share their expertise, but in fact the problem is that they try to be in control. The academics' reflex response is to do more research, and this will utterly frustrate the managers. I've heard managers many times complaining 'I've got to do something out there with the species today. You guys have all this information and expertise. I want to do the best job I can. But for you to tell me that I have to sit and twiddle my thumbs for five years while you do more studies is unacceptable.' I came out of an academic background, but I was fortunate that over the years I have spent a lot of time working with managers. I came to respect their integrity. If species are going to be saved, these are the guys that are going to do it."

Seal's focus was clear: find ways to build better scientific knowledge through collaboration and find ways to put the power in the hands of those who could make the change. He began by working with zoos, to build information systems and collaboration. Then, in 1979, Seal took on the chairmanship of the Captive Breeding Specialist Group (CBSG), a subcommittee of the huge, voluntary, science-driven International Union for the Conservation of Nature, a Switzerland-based organization. Seal recruited a huge network of committed scientists to work with him on a voluntary basis. He then set about designing workshops that would equalize power, putting zoo directors, wildlife managers, scientists and NGO activists on the same footing. These workshops were called Population and Habitat Viability Assessments (PHVAs), and they turned traditional power arrangements on their head. "The very structure of the workshop sets power aside as an issue," Seal observed. "I open with a statement that people are there because they share a common interest in the species. I also underline that they all have expertise and expert knowledge which is going to add value to the process of determining just how endangered the species is. I then point out that they are all going to be handicapped by the fact that they represent different interests. By and large I have been successful at that. Sometimes it takes a lot of effort to make sure all the key players are in the room. Then I work to remove the power issue entirely."

At the workshops, Seal and collaborators facilitated intensive information exchange and action planning. Under pressure of time, all information sources, whether scientific studies, field notes or observations gathered from local hunters or villagers, were used to make assessments about the health and viability of the species. Then, based on these assessments, joint recommendations for action were created. The demand for these workshops all over the world increased steadily.

"It gets easier all the time," Seal confided. "The fact is that there is an enormous satisfaction on people's part in producing things and seeing that their activities are useful. They meet people, tackle problems, and line up resources. We work in small groups and produce reports. This process has been an enormously powerful tool for producing consensus."

Seal's and CBSG's initiatives have had great impact. As one observer put it, "If Seal and his team showed up to analyze panther problems, there would be no nonsense. They would not be influenced by factional interests or provincial views."[10] Seal was able to equalize power in the workshop context and to ensure the power to make decisions was in the hands of the scientists and the wildlife managers. To avoid pressure for particular outcomes, and to keep the process from becoming bogged down in bureaucratic red tape, Seal avoided working with powerful funding agencies. As he said, "I can afford not to [accept that kind of funding] because I'm not looking for a billion-dollar activity . . . I'm not dependent on any single institution or group for my professional expertise. I'm not dependent on any single government for activities. If we lose a whole country that isn't willing to participate it doesn't make any difference. I've got five more standing in line to take their place."

Seal actually preferred to work on a shoestring, sometimes investing his own cash to keep things going. His richest resource was the tremendous personal and professional loyalty he garnered. He made the volunteer scientists who worked with him feel that their capabilities were connected with huge possibilities; that what they did made a huge difference. Scientists found that a little input would go a long way when working with CBSG, and that the normal obstacles to innovation were somehow removed. A new technique or process introduced in a workshop in one country would be picked up and used in other parts of the world within weeks. For that reason, people were willing to donate their time and expertise. "We've discovered that academia is waiting to be mined," one CBSG member said. "The world's top-ranking population biologists like to do something altruistic once in a while. You can call the best geneticist alive, and say, 'We're going to have a meeting on the Florida panther,' and he'll say, 'Oh yes, I have the papers, there are only twenty-five left.' I'll say, 'We'll buy you a ticket, put you up, we need some expertise.' He says, 'Sure!' You've just got two days of the world's best geneticist at no charge."

Seal worked hard to protect those in his circle of influence from interference. This was not always easy, as the professionals who became involved could be accused of diverting their time and energy from their own organizations. But Seal had an unusual approach to dealing with the powerful stranger. He had been a powerful scientist in his own right, and he knew how to talk to people in power. Seal took the time to connect meaningfully to the power players, such as the zoo directors and foundation heads, who helped to support the core work of the CBSG. In his travels he was endlessly patient when working with the dignitaries and officials who came to open his workshops. And when he met opposition, he tried hard to avoid open conflict, deliberately side-stepping it. He tried to work below the radar, avoiding publicity if possible. Ultimately, he didn't see the hope of real change as residing in his hands; the hope for change lay, he felt, in the younger people he met. He felt these young people should be connected to each other, and when he encountered enthusiastic responses he would invite people, on the spot, to upcoming workshops in distant countries. This created a sometimes chaotic travelling road show, but it paid dividends. A number of these individuals became drivers of new initiatives.

Seal's approach was definitely "sticky." It attracted people who would work long and hard, both to save a valued species and to be part of this effective and exciting community, which was a "battery recharger," as one volunteer attested. Interestingly, as Seal's efforts began to show results and, as the network grew, he started to win acclaim and awards. These he resisted. It was not unusual for him to accept international awards with a curt "Thank you," skipping the traditional speech. He saw recognition of this nature as a kind of temptation, a way in which a leader might become misled into thinking that he was the source of power in the system. He believed, instead, that the power lay in the kinds of connections between people that he repeatedly tried to forge and nurture. In the new connections, the changed relationships, lay the power for transforming systems. For CBSG such connections were the lifeblood of a worldwide collaboration to save endangered species. But sometimes confrontation is also key to transformation.

—

Mary Gordon has become a Canadian icon. Elected an Ashoka Fellow in 2002 for her creative work, she is red-headed and vibrant with a quick wit and a lovely singing voice. But what has made her internationally famous are her attempts to eradicate bullying in our schools.[11]

Gordon grew up in Newfoundland, in a large and boisterous family that was very concerned with citizen engagement and with social justice. "My father had a huge sense of social justice," she says, "and he very much alerted us to the fact that there were children that didn't land as lucky as we did. There was a lot of poverty where I grew up, and we were just middle class; we weren't rich but when I would bring home friends who were really, really poor and smelly, my mother would treat them just as anyone else who was a guest in our home. I remember visiting the home of one young girl—I was teased about playing with her because she was smelly—and the baby was in the sink. I wouldn't be criticizing but I was astonished. But my mother said that whenever you go into someone's home remember it is their castle and treat it as such."

After graduating from college, Gordon became a kindergarten teacher. From her first days in the classroom she was struck by the importance of involving families in a child's education, since parents, in her view, had the most power to shape the future for their children. But schools weren't set up for the kind of family engagement Gordon had in mind.

She started a program on family literacy and went out to the streets to bring people in. She went to laundromats and diners, anywhere she thought help was needed and there were obstacles to providing it. For example, for many immigrant women, their own mothers-in-law represented a barrier to them becoming involved in Gordon's literacy efforts. Since they couldn't speak English themselves, they had no idea what their daughters-in-law would be reading and were suspicious of the texts themselves. So Gordon got the material translated. She had no budget so she did it piecemeal, even asking taxi drivers stopped at red lights to translate paragraphs for her. She would then give the translated texts to the young women and say, "Give it to your mother-in-law. She can read it, right? Then let's ask her to come to the program."

And she brought people in.

In the 1980s she shifted her focus to teenage parents, as she came to believe that they were the ones most in need of support and there was little of it to be had. "I went to children's aid, I went to public health, I went to all of the people who knew about social problems and they said, 'You will never get teenage mothers to come out. They just won't come,'" Gordon recalls. "So I went to the teenage mothers instead of the expert . . . I mean it was the principle of empathy, right, put yourself in the other's shoes. I rode the elevators that teenage mothers ride. I spoke to the teenage mothers as a person, not as a helper, not as an expert, not as a worker. Because I believed that to change what's going to happen, it would have to be guided by the people who had an investment in change. Not me. I needed to listen rather than preach." Gordon even hung out in banks where teenage mothers came to cash their welfare cheques, and she asked questions and she listened.

Her idea was that if these teenage mothers could bring their children into the classroom, they could help create a new dynamic. Children at risk for such pregnancies themselves could witness first-hand the care it takes to raise a child. Perhaps this would prevent them from becoming teenage parents. But there were other unexpected benefits of the work. Gordon says, "We ask parents to bring the babies in when they are about two months old. They put them on a blanket on the floor . . . a beached whale on the floor. And I put my hands on the baby and I say, 'Is Jamie alright? Jamie can't talk, children, so look at Jamie's body and face and tell me, is Jamie saying yes or no?' It's about respect for the body, respect for the will of the child, don't break the will, respect it and listen to it."

Gordon believed that if children developed their capacity for empathy with babies, they would be less likely to bully those who were younger and weaker than themselves. For Gordon, this was all about power and changing the flow of power through changing relationships. She was no stranger to the idea of scalar invariance: bullying was rooted in every scale of the social order. "You have relationships of power within corporations, and within legal systems," she says. "When you have an imbalance, and no mutuality in relationship, you have abuse. You have bullying in most businesses, in most teacher-student relationships. And it all gets kicked down to the kids. You keep coming down and down. You come down to the school system, you come down to the family structure and you come down to the kids. I'm not interested in the corporations . . . let them battle it out, because they will. Governments will battle it out. Communities at the municipal level will battle it out. But when you get to the level of the two main social institutions in the world, families and schools, that's where we have to teach consensus building rather than power mongering."

She called her program Roots of Empathy, and her goal was to turn the hierarchy on its head. She designed it to be respectful of the least powerful, the baby. The whole experience is based on letting the baby lead. And the program has shown real results. From the beginning of Roots of Empathy she engaged scientists as evaluators to measure the program's impact. The results have been startling. When the researchers compared children who were involved in the Roots of Empathy Program and those who weren't, they found that children who had taken the program were more socially sensitive, showed insight into their own emotions and those of others, were more social and less aggressive. The incidence of bullying dropped.

Mary Gordon sees this as a sea change. Change those relationships at the base of all human interactions and perhaps there will be a cascade effect so that violence and power abuse will diminish throughout the whole system.

But why and how do these simple interactions work to reduce aggression? Gordon's theory is that "children who have a lot of punitive relationships in their lives are power hungry, they want to get even." The term "power hungry," when applied to young children, seems paradoxical. It suggests that those to whom no power is given become starved for power, like they might be starved for food. The solution for Gordon was equally paradoxical: give children a chance to care for those weaker than themselves, and this will feed them, making them less starved for power and less in need of aggression and bullying.

"In one classroom, there was a seven-year-old boy who exhibited extremely aggressive and anti-social behaviour," she recounts. "Tom would come to class with a hat pulled down over his eyes and he never smiled. In and out of foster homes for many years, this young boy was very lonely and very angry. Mean to his classmates, belligerent, disruptive in class—he had no friends. When the Roots of Empathy instructor, parent and baby entered the classroom, the teacher was very concerned that Tom might harm the baby. Upon the advice of ROE staff, he was placed right next to the baby. Imagine Tom's reaction when the baby smiled at him. During the first class visit, the boy smiled and interacted with the infant. During the second visit, he took off his hat when he was near the baby. And, at the third visit, he brought a dirty pink feather to tickle the bottom of the baby's feet. This young boy was learning to empathize with the baby. From that point on, his teacher and his fellow classmates saw him from a new and kinder perspective. He became integrated into the social life of the classroom through Roots of Empathy."

Gordon's idea of empathy is a complement to the Greek notion of nemesis. For the Greeks, nemesis was a goddess, the personification of divine justice. The word refers to any disturbance of due proportion—whether good or bad—in the distribution of fortune. Like Carl Jung's "shadow," the idea captures the haunting dangers of extremes. When an individual behaves in a way that is either too good or too bad it suggests that he has repressed, edited out, or rejected parts of his human nature. Both the bully and the saint have lost a sense of proportion. In some sense, like Yeats's fanatic, such a person is "maimed" and not fully human. In Gordon's view, so is the bully.

The Greeks believed that ultimately and inevitably, if not reclaimed, or owned, we would meet our nemesis and it would destroy us. So the person who cannot identify or empathize with weakness becomes a bully, and her rage at weakness will ultimately destroy her. The person who cannot identify with violence becomes a coward; and his fear in the face of aggression will ultimately destroy him. Having lost our ability to recognize ourselves in the other (the roots of empathy), our own behaviour also becomes increasingly rigid. The only solution is to reclaim, through insight or through identification, our lost or repressed capacities.

All of us are prey to some extent to these kinds of distortions. Try this experiment. Think of someone you know who irritates you unreasonably. We'll call him Marvin. Most people you can deal with, but Marvin gets on your nerves like fingernails on a blackboard. Now on a piece of paper write down a list of adjectives that describe Marvin's irritating qualities. Don't try to moderate your description: be as critical as you sometimes feel.

Now, in a second list, right beside the first, write the opposite quality. If the first item on your Marvin list is "stingy," write "generous." If the second item is "cowardly," write "brave" and so on. When you have listed the opposite term for each quality, read that second list out loud. Do you feel a shock of recognition? Generally, that second list turns out to include those qualities one feels most proud of in oneself. This exercise should give us some insight into our disproportionate irritation with Marvin. If we have worked so hard to be generous, we have had to repress all inclination in ourselves to be stingy. If what we most admire is bravery, we will be hard on any tendency toward cowardly behaviour in ourselves or others. Eventually we may forget that we ever felt stingy or cowardly. Worse, we become limited in our own repertoire of responses. There are times, after all, when being stingy is appropriate, and there are times when it is good to be a coward. Of course, we would be more likely to call these qualities parsimony and circumspection when we apply them to ourselves. But we all are strengthened, are made more powerful and effective, by possessing the full range of human responses.

Roots of Empathy works to keep us whole. The child who is treated as worthless becomes starved for power. He learns to repress all weakness and to disdain it as he himself was disdained. But perhaps, if caught early enough he can be taught, like Tom, to make friends with his own weakness as he makes friends with the baby, and this makes him whole again. Whole people are perhaps not as likely to grow into bullies—to bully requires being maimed. To bully is a disproportionate response.

In exploring the dynamics of bullying, Gordon arrived at profound insights about the need to engage power to create change. Her approach was direct. Working at the scale of family and classroom relationships, she brought the weak and the powerful together, and built connection through empathy. Her work has resonance with such twentieth-century global initiatives as the Truth and Reconciliation Commission (TRC) in South Africa.[12]

An innovative and courageous political process launched in 1995, the TRC was headed by Archbishop Desmond Tutu. After a thirty-five year history of legally sanctioned racism, the world had witnessed the birth of the "rainbow" nation, where racism was outlawed. But the difficult process of healing had only begun. As evidence of atrocities committed by whites and blacks mounted, the challenge of holding on to a belief that one group held the "truth" and "good" while the other was full of deceit and evil was increasingly difficult. Energy, even determination, was required to maintain the stereotypes, and Tutu knew that this energy needed to be released so it could be reinvested in a transformed and reorganized society.

The TRC was a bold attempt to create a safe container to release the rage and the hurt. The encounter was internal as well; citizens had to face the mirror, to look deeply into their own actions and seek forgiveness for their complicity in the atrocities that had occurred during their watch. Hearings were organized to bring people and groups who had been enemies for decades face to face. Enemies were confronted, talked to, listened to and, often, wept with. The encounters were very difficult, but those who attended and observed the hearings saw many examples of profoundly changed relationships.

The confrontation engendered by the TRC has become something of a model for how to overcome long-standing acrimony. Social innovators in the Aboriginal community in Canada and elsewhere have considered using it as a framework. However, the TRC in South Africa has been only a step in the process; real and enduring balance has yet to be achieved. Having joined hands across the chasm, a sense of unity and a new commitment for change is created. But that alone does not shake loose the resources "locked" into the status quo. In fact, it often signals a period of protracted conflict as those with resources, those at the hubs, seek to maintain their control. In some cases, revolt or revolution precipitates a sudden shift (as in the French Revolution). In many cases of social transformation, however, the shift is less visible, less dramatic, but no less profound, involving reaching hands across another chasm, separating the haves and have-nots, and in doing so reconfiguring the power distribution. After confrontation, how do we build collaboration between those who want change and those who hold the resources to sustain that change?

—

Palliative care, as a movement, began in the early 1950s. At that time hospital care in the West was dominated by a medical/scientific approach, which focused on cures rather than care. Medical technologies, pharmacological innovations and surgical techniques radically improved the curative potential of medical practice. Hospitals increasingly became places where the science of medicine (and latterly the technology of medicine) was practised. Incurable, dying patients were a problem to the hospitals, which were poorly equipped to handle them—both physically and philosophically. The inability to cure was seen to be a failure of medicine. Curative care had trapped the resources of medicine by capturing the attention of funders, governments, health care policy makers, hospital administrators, medical schools, physicians and the media. Stories of health care cures were reported in the newspapers; the more dramatic the cure, the more likely the coverage.

As a young woman, Cicely Saunders decided to challenge this trend.[13] Her own experience, working as a nurse in England after World War II, convinced her that the dying needed special treatment: "not only better pain control but better overall care." She argued that "people needed the space to be themselves. I coined the term 'total pain,' from my understanding that dying people have physical, spiritual, psychological, and social pain that must be treated. I have been working on that ever since."

A deeply religious Anglican, Saunders saw the mission to improve the conditions of the dying as a calling. It was so strong that she began volunteering as a nurse at homes for the dying after work, and eventually entered medical school at the age of thirty-three. Once she graduated she focused her practice on the needs of the dying and their families, and to developing an approach that came to be known as palliative care.

"Palliative" comes from the Latin *pallium,* meaning a cloak. "In palliative care, symptoms are 'cloaked' with treatments whose primary or sole aim is to promote patients' comfort. Palliative care, however, extends far beyond symptom relief. Its existence is poignantly reflected in a sentence from the Qur'an [Koran]: 'May you be wrapped in tenderness, you my brother, as if in a cloak.'"[14]

The concept of palliative care came as a godsend to those dying in hospitals, but it flew in the face of the medical establishment's emphasis on cure. Saunders set about to raise the consciousness of the medical establishment. It was uphill work. To the proponents of cure, palliative care seemed anti-progress, a poor cousin to modern medicine. Saunders toured and lectured relentlessly, however, and like Ulysses Seal she found converts on the front lines. Many doctors and nurses had grown disenchanted with the emphasis on cure alone. They had seen too many of their patients and their families suffering unnecessarily; they had seen the medical profession turn its back on the dying. Saunders's initiatives, like those of Elizabeth Kübler-Ross, who wrote about the stages of dying, were greeted with relief, even gratitude. Lecture halls were packed. But the practitioners who sought to set up palliative care units within hospitals still faced resistance from those who controlled the resources. Particular strategies were needed to turn these skeptics into collaborators.

One of the leaders in the movement in Canada, Dr. Balfour Mount, introduced the country's first palliative care unit right in the fortress of the powerful stranger—one of Canada's largest teaching hospitals, the Royal Victoria in Montreal.[15] Mount had suffered from and survived cancer while he was an intern, and this contributed to his decision to become a surgeon, and a urologist specializing in cancer. When he chose to leave surgery to focus on palliative care, it came as a shock to those who worked with him. As one senior surgeon later said, "When Bal left, I felt that we'd lost a good surgeon and we lost something more. We lost the kind of radical urology which we've never got back again . . . He brought an innovative orientation even then. At the time I tried to convince him not to leave [surgery]. I thought he would never make a career out of it [palliative care]. How wrong can you get?"

Mount had become convinced of the need for palliative care, but he needed clear data, not anecdotes. In 1973 he initiated a survey of dying patients and their caregivers in the hospital. The results revealed that many patients were dying in physical and psychological pain, and caregivers felt that not all that was necessary was being done. Mount had heard of Saunders's work and travelled to England to speak to her. He was convinced by what he saw there—a radical approach (by the standards of teaching hospitals) of putting the patient first. "Basically, palliative care means to focus on the whole person rather than simply on the biology of disease," Mount explained. "To focus on the patient and the family rather than just the patient. To focus on home care rather than institution care. To restructure the health care teams so that they weren't hierarchical and physician dominated."

In the institutional culture of an elite teaching hospital, this represented a radical innovation. Mount had the support of many of the young doctors and medical students, but to create a palliative care centre he had to convince the hierarchy. In the world of the hospital the chief resource was beds, and these were jealously guarded by heads of departments. Any new unit had to take beds from existing units, which could not be done without the support of those in power. The very notion of allocating beds to palliative care in a teaching hospital focused on research and cure was close to heresy. And this was just the beginning. Palliative care also demanded a team approach where doctors were equals with nurses, therapists, psychologists. It demanded the inclusion of volunteers and families in the care process itself. As the head of volunteers said, "Many of my volunteers were professionals with considerable personal experience . . . many were more educated than the nurses and the nurses found them a threat."

Mount's approach to winning the resources he needed was very close to that of the HIV/AIDS advocates in our opening parable—he worked hard to build collaboration and he succeeded by building identification between the palliative care concept and key concerns of those in power. He had a clear idea how to proceed: "When I am intent on getting something, I don't spend time complaining. I look at how things work. I learned from childhood that I could convince people if I believed in it myself. So I looked around and realized there were two to three people who had to be convinced because they controlled the decision-making process."

The three key people were the chief of surgery, the chief of professional services and the head of nursing. Even if they were initially unsure about the place of palliative care in a teaching hospital, these three people held Mount in considerable respect because of his track record as a surgeon. And Mount respected them and worked hard to connect to their particular interests and passions. The head of nursing, who described herself as very interested in organizational politics, praised Mount as a "master politician." Mount sold her on the idea of palliative care as a team approach with a special role for nursing. The chief of surgery had long admired Mount's surgical abilities, but was skeptical when he abandoned surgery to take up the cause of palliative care. He had deep respect for research, however, and Mount convinced him that an experimental palliative care unit was an ideal site for research into pain control among other things. The chief of professional services, a deeply religious man, was attracted to the whole-patient approach, which, at least in the hospice movement in England, was deeply rooted in Christian ideals of service. The key people saw the palliative care initiative as a window of opportunity, a means of realizing their own priorities. So they supported the release of resources, or at least did not oppose it.

As one doctor said, "The secret of his success was that he hooked into something spiritual, something emotional, something idealistic, which is in most doctors. Many were suspicious, but Mount packaged it in a way that was scientifically and intellectually acceptable. There are a lot of people who get you crying, but in the cold light of day you say: 'How can I support this?' Mount took great care to speak the language of his audience at all times. Whether an individual needed scientific language, political language or spiritual language, Mount was able to identify that and use it to link people to his larger purpose."

Mount's approach tells us much about engaging the powerful stranger, knowing and being known. He had confronted the powerful stranger within in the form of his own illness. He could identify with the dying patients and their families. But he also had a foot in the world of the elite medical hierarchy—he understood what made that world tick. While many explicitly recognized Mount's powers of persuasion and his political skills, people did not feel manipulated. Mount did not create an appetite for change; he tapped a deep-seated desire for change. He did not fool people into supporting his initiative; he made them realize it was an opportunity for moving forward a range of cherished agendas. Then, having secured the initial resources, Mount took care to design the initiative so that it could, over time, build collaboration with a broad group of doctors. As a physician team member recalled:

> At the beginning, the first patients came from inside the
> hospital. We feared resistance and there was some, despite
> the fact that the Vic is a hospital that is geared for innovation.
> Mount spent a lot of time thinking about how to sell
> palliative care to the hospital, how to make it palatable and
> how not to threaten anyone. He left the options open so that
> the doctors could refer patients to the unit without losing
> them. He presented it as a supplement and a complement to
> their services. He also created a policy committee with key
> doctors on it; those with big cancer loads so that they wouldn't
> be threatened. Mount was a specialist in a specialist's world.
> I am a G.P. and could never have done it.

The palliative care unit at the Royal Victoria hospital went on to be a model for other such units in Canada and around the world. Many attribute its success to Mount. Certainly, like many social innovators we have encountered in this book, he was prepared to work tirelessly for what he believed. Mount himself, however, tells the story as one of almost miraculous coincidences and opportunities: his encounters with Saunders, the people who joined his team, the willingness of the Royal Victoria to support innovation; the resources of time and energy that flowed his way. While power and the powerful stranger can be seen as locked up in the established structures of the old system—inaccessible to those who wish to change things—the opposite is also true: power is a wave, which once released can carry the social innovator forward like a sailing ship. To paraphrase Niels Bohr, the physicist best known for his analysis of the microstructure of atoms, there are two kinds of truth—superficial truths, the opposite of which are obviously wrong, and profound truths, whose opposites are equally right. The powerful stranger is not friend *or* foe—she is both.

How to Engage the Powerful Stranger

This chapter offers ideas at both the personal and the systems levels for bringing about changed power relationships. These two levels of change overlap and intertwine. In order to identify and confront the powerful stranger, our actions are drawn from the three steps developed throughout this chapter. The first step is the development of connections and group ties. The second is confrontation, with the power in others and in ourselves. The third is learning how to collaborate with powerful allies. Each of these requires both skills and seeing things in relationship or in context. Transformation needs to occur at all three levels for real change to happen.

One of the challenges facing those who wish to transform society is that money and power are so often linked. And those who fund or support social innovation are not always comfortable discussing this relationship. The philanthropist we introduced in Chapter 2, for example, is visibly uncomfortable with the explicit analysis of power. The trustees of her philanthropic foundation are part of the existing power structure, as she is herself. Social innovation involves—indeed, requires—redistributing power. It's all well and good to talk about curing diseases, supporting social innovation, changing poor neighbourhoods, improving education, stimulating economic development, sustaining the environment—but changing the distribution of power? Why would those with wealth and power want to support that?

When funders and grantees encounter each other, it's hard enough to talk frankly about money, but power is the philanthropic taboo. So the first strategic calculation the social innovator must make in this regard is how explicit to be. Should he pretend that power isn't a central issue and honour the taboo, or make the agenda of transforming power relationships explicit and confront it with funders? If talking with a philanthropist who supports social innovation, we would offer this advice:

• In any discussion of power and its redistribution, link the issue directly to the organization's mission and keep it in that context.

Any philanthropic foundation envisions change of some kind, otherwise, why exist at all? This opens the door for the staff and board of a foundation to discuss how the hoped-for changes would likely be brought about. Such discussions are often simplistic. But they don't have to be. A complex systems approach to thinking about mission fulfillment changes all that. Using the framework presented throughout this book to consider mission fulfillment will involve looking at the foundation's role and function in the existing system and what kinds of changed relationships would be necessary to support genuine social transformation.

Power isn't the starting point in such a discussion, but if the conversation reaches any depth, power dynamics will surface in connection to mission fulfillment, which is appropriate; there it will challenge those in power to examine the depth of their commitment to real change. The powerful stranger for a foundation may, then, be its own board of trustees. This is not an easy, one-time discussion. But this process can energize and take to a new level what are otherwise often pretty tame board meetings. The purpose is to prepare a philanthropic board to stay the course when the social innovations they support start to generate both real changes and inevitable resistance to those changes when the powerful status quo pushes back. The film *Kinsey* portrays how, a half-century ago, the Rockefeller Foundation withdrew its funding for research on sexuality when powerful national politicians attacked it. That's a useful scenario for boards to consider when asking whether and how they might respond differently and when thinking through contemporary scenarios linked to real social innovations.

—

In contrast to philanthropy, power discussions are anything but taboo in the government sector; politics is all about power. But politicians are much more interested in gaining power than sharing it, despite campaign rhetoric to the contrary. Politicians are especially prone to thinking you're either with us or against us. From the perspective of the social innovator, those in political power may be the powerful strangers, but from the perspective of those who hold political power, the reverse is true. What would this lead us to say in conversation with policy makers?

• Invite social innovators to the table. Whether what they propose is in line with your preferences or not, they are valuable sources of grassroots information about trends, potential tipping points and new directions in the political economy. Treat them respectfully as information allies.

This advice attempts to spin a win-win scenario for policy makers and social innovators around their common need for information. Each needs to respect and understand the other. No, they won't naively share everything they're thinking about and all that they know, but what people in power, especially politicians, know a lot about is negotiating. You have to give something to get something. We urge policy makers to treat social innovators as weathervanes that can show them which way the wind is blowing. And those powerful strangers, the social innovators who want to change the status quo, may turn out to be allies after all.

The implications of the powerful stranger for the voluntary or non-profit sector are especially profound. While it is obvious that philanthropic foundations and politicians may be powerful strangers for social innovators, those dedicated to serving the needs of the less fortunate might appear to be natural power allies. But precisely because so many not-for-profit organizations live so close to the edge of survival, they are especially attuned to threats from new actors and innovations that might undermine their already tenuous place in the power and resource pecking order.

• Become skilled in and sophisticated about power dynamics. Hone your skills by seeking out and engaging with those in power. Make yourself, and therefore your organization, a serious player and worthy ally in support of social innovation.

The example of Ulysses Seal and his leadership in the Captive Breeding Specialist Group offers much to emulate and inspire in this regard.

Recall that he took the time to connect meaningfully to the power players, such as the zoo directors and foundation heads, who were critical to CBSG's core work. He cultivated dignitaries and officials around the world as necessary. When he encountered resistance, generally based on a perception that he had invaded other people's turf, he worked to minimize antagonism. Especially worthy of reflection was his funding approach. He didn't apply to the big international agencies—obvious and with deep pockets—because he didn't want the strings attached to such funding. Instead, he focused on harvesting the energy and time of professionals who shared his vision; they were his chief resource. He engaged with power hierarchies as much as was required to protect those resources. He understood that by creating connections among the committed, even if these were not the power brokers, he built a foundation for powerful change that might ultimately result in the redistribution of power.

Astute social innovators, like Balfour Mount, tap into the existing rules, systems, values and networks—many hidden from view—and turn them into resources for change. Gain access to the power brokers, and the pattern of resource flow may suddenly shift. When that occurs, the innovation has the resources to take root, to become a different way of doing things. But, as noted, a new threat often becomes apparent: that of being seduced into becoming the new establishment, shoring up one's own claim to resources, raising the drawbridge and becoming in turn the powerful stranger to someone else's innovation.

We once again end the chapter by speaking to those who are trying to figure out where and how they can make a difference. What do we have to say to them about encounters with powerful strangers?

- Be thoughtful and reflective about your place and role in the power dynamics that are part of your world. Become more skillful and sophisticated in assessing the role of power and connecting to those who have power. Understand that power is a two-edged sword that can be used to both resist and foment change.
- Engaging in social innovation can sometimes be frightening, as you confront the hostility of those who oppose change, or you seek to build connections, first to those like yourself, then to those with many more resources than yourself. Remember that linking with those like yourself builds momentum, but ultimately you may need to build bridges between your movement and those who support the status quo. Look for openings to collaborate while staying true to your own desire to see change happen.

Power is still experienced by most of us as a game of haves and have-nots. Whether you have power or you don't, chances are that you need to confront your own fanatic heart—your suspicions of and anger with the other. To release new energy, your own or that of others, you need to empathize with the other (and your own potential for otherness) and reclaim their sentiments as your own. You need to find the roots of empathy.

You do not have to be good.
You do not have to walk on your knees
for a hundred miles through the desert, repenting.
You only have to let the soft animal of your body
love what it loves.
Tell me about despair, yours, and I will tell you mine.
Meanwhile the world goes on.
Meanwhile the sun and the clear pebbles of the rain
are moving across the landscapes,
over the prairies and the deep trees,
the mountains and the rivers.
Meanwhile the wild geese, high in the clean blue air,
are heading home again.
Whoever you are, no matter how lonely,
the world offers itself to your imagination,
calls to you like the wild geese, harsh and exciting—
over and over announcing your place
in the family of things.

Mary Oliver, "Wild Geese"

5. Let It Find You

When Bob Geldof made the decision to try to organize the Live Aid concert, he had a curious experience. He found that momentum built almost faster than he could organize it. Everything he did seemed to work. "I am not a great believer in the notions of coincidence, serendipity, synchronicity and the other rag, tag and bobtail of karmic law, but some things seemed too easy . . . Hundreds of people dropping everything and concentrating on this one thing," Geldof wrote. "No one particularly stood in my way; on the contrary, doors impenetrable a week earlier swung open effortlessly."[1]

What Geldof describes is the other face of power, a face that social innovators recognize and count on. At times power is a stranger, who must be managed and engaged. At times, however, it is a torrent, which the social innovator rides as best she can. David Wagoner hints at this with the concluding line of his poem "Lost": "you must let it find you." But that phrase makes it sound more of a choice than it feels to most of the social innovators we encountered. Almost without exception, the social innovators we talked to describe a moment in the process when they themselves felt swept along by the stream, caught up by forces they may have triggered but that they in no sense felt they controlled. Momentum can build to an intensity that surprises the people who dreamed of such a transformation.

This is, in fact, good news. It means that the energy to create transformation lies outside the social innovator, waiting to be tapped. "You do not have to walk on your knees / for a hundred miles through the desert," writes Mary Oliver. You can let go, let the energy carry you. There are forces in the natural order of things that are the real source of transformation. This is the other side of power.

Bob Geldof's effort alone, although critical, was far from enough to unleash the tide of contributions that marked both Band Aid and the Live Aid concert, and yet the tide was unleashed. Balfour Mount similarly remembered that while launching his ground-breaking palliative care unit, "There were all sorts of providential things, remarkable coincidences that changed forever my concept of how these things happen." In complexity science this is called emergence, a term used to describe things that are unpredictable, which seem to result from the interactions between elements, and are outside any one agent's control.

Many social innovators ask themselves questions: How does the momentum for the work build? What is my role as momentum builds? How do I ride this flood of resources? Can I trust the natural flow and energy? What if I can't control them? What do I need to do to trust the flow? How do I let it find me?

The fact that emergent experiences happen regularly to social innovators can be an indicator that the time is right. But that doesn't tell us how to anticipate or even capitalize on such experiences. For that, we need to look more closely at the experience itself, and at the underlying conditions that seem to produce it.

—

The Czech psychologist and author Mihaly Csikszentmihalyi is fascinated by peak or optimal human experiences. In his early work, he studied people who devoted enormous number of hours to an activity that required discipline and yet was not rewarded by money or fame. What drove musicians, composers, dancers, athletes, chess players in their tireless pursuits, he wondered? In latter years, his work has expanded to include a wider variety of creative individuals, including business leaders, politicians, social activists and scientists. Through intensive interviews and rigorous observations, he has done more than anyone else in recent memory to detail and explore the optimal experiences that motivate such creators. He calls such experiences "finding flow."[2]

Flow is difficult to define, but Csikszentmihalyi says it is characterized by "the sense of effortless action that stands out as the best [approach]. [The] person in flow is completely focused. There is no space in consciousness for distracting thoughts. The sense of time is distorted: hours seem to pass by in minutes. When a person's entire being is stretched in the full functioning of body and mind, whatever one does becomes worth doing for its own sake; living becomes its own justification."[3]

For Csikszentmihalyi, finding flow is a psychological state, very much within the capacity of the individual to create, if not to control. He associates it with creativity, but also with situations in which goals are clear, feedback is immediate and skills are stretched. This kind of experience has certainly been described by "virtuosi" in disciplines from athletics to mysticism. One of the most clear-cut descriptions of flow is by Edwin Land, the inventor of Polaroid instant photography. Describing his periods of invention, he says, "I find it is very important to work intensively for long hours when I am beginning to see solutions to a problem. At such times atavistic competences seem to come welling up. You are handling so many variables at a barely conscious level that you can't afford to be interrupted. If you are, it may take a year to cover the same ground you could cover otherwise in sixty hours."[4] In this vivid description we see the connection between creativity, skill and thought processes at work.

But for social innovators such as Geldof, flow occurs not so much internally as externally—in the relationship between their own activity and that of others. This is an experience that is perhaps best equated to those moments in team sports or in the theatre when the individual player is so caught up in the performance of the group that he performs at levels beyond his apparent skills. And it feels almost effortless. This is more than teamwork. It has to do with practice and with skill on the part of all the players, but when such magic moments occur, they create something alive, unique and totally involving. The divisions between audience and actors seem to dissolve and all are brought into a world made anew.

When social innovations take flight, they have this same sense of two-way flow—the innovators are influencing their context while their context is influencing them in an endless to and fro. Decisions are made, actions are taken but it is not always clear how they came about. There is a wonderful sense of collective ownership: all who are involved feel this is their project, their cause, their time to change the world. Jeff Brown and his colleagues experienced this flow when citizens, street youth, pastors and police all began to work together to improve their community, a moment when they stopped pointing fingers at each other and began to look at their own complicity and responsibility, and at what bound them all together.

These moments of flow always have something magical about them. Indeed, the sociologist Emile Durkheim called the experience "collective effervescence." He described such effervescence as a natural by-product of the patterns of interaction that occur between people, which "attain their greatest intensity at the moment when [they] are assembled together and are in immediate relations with one another, when they all partake of the same idea and the same sentiments."[5] He argued that there is something about the patterns of interaction, of being together, which in themselves generate an unusual level of energy. This energy is stirred by sharing a common idea and a common sense of purpose.

Durkheim's work formed the basis for the understanding of crowd behaviour in the early twentieth century. More recently, complexity science has suggested that the source of flow may be biochemical as well as social. Steven Johnson, in his book *Emergence*, describes the mysteries of slime moulds, which are single-celled organisms when food is plentiful and multicelled organisms when food is in short supply.[6] As multicelled entities, they can move more quickly to other areas to look for food sources. When food is plentiful again, they separate and become single-celled organisms again. For many years, the dominant theory of slime moulds was that a pacemaker cell controlled this behaviour, stimulating the production of a pheromone that brought cells together. The fact that the pacemaker cells could not be found did not deter scientists from the theory. They blamed their failure on insufficient data or poorly designed experiments.

But scientist Evelyn Keller eventually asked, in 1968, what if there are no pacemakers? What if slime mould comes together and falls apart without central control? Then she showed how it could work. If individual cells had the capacity to both emit the pheromone and sense its existence, they could start and stop production of the pheromone themselves. In some ways, you could see this as operating like a furnace with a thermostat. When the room temperature near the thermostat reaches a set temperature, the furnace shuts off and starts again only when the temperature drops below another set level. For slime moulds, each cell has its own thermostat and furnace. Each cell knows when it is time to produce more of the pheromone and when it is time to come together. Rather than relying on a central controller to determine when food is in short supply, the responsibility is distributed among all cells, each of which assesses its local conditions. When a cell is unable to find sufficient food in its local environment, it emits the pheromone and other cells can follow the trail of this substance. When several cells emit the pheromone, they cluster together by following each others' trails, serving both their self-interest and their collective interest in survival. Global conditions are assessed not by a higher authority but by thousands of individual local sensors.

It took more than thirty years for Keller's theory to become widely accepted. Bottom-up behaviour seems illogical to Western minds because we have a hierarchical bias against self-organization. We display this same bias in our common understanding of how human change happens, especially in organizations. Our popular management magazines are filled with stories of the omniscient CEO or leader who can see the opportunities or threats in the environment and leads the people into the light. As a society, we are most comfortable with the explanation of the pacemaker cell—the leader who figures it all out and lets the followers know the truth and the path. Because of our dominant belief in the omniscient and visionary leader, we often miss the other partner in the dance of change—the self-organization that is so critical to achieving flow.

The paradox in our quest for social innovation is to neither ignore the individual leaders nor let them dominate our analysis to such an extent that we miss the self-organization—the capacity of individual players to both assess their local context and act in ways that create a global pattern. Unlike slime mould, humans do not have pre-set sensors that trigger specific social behaviours. However, we respond to communication; verbal, written and body languages are used to convey intentions, understanding, emotions and values. A leader often intensifies or clarifies communication. In this sense she may act as a powerful attractor. But unless the communication resonates at some level with local experience, the self-organizing pattern—or flow—will not emerge.

Can we deliberately enhance the sensitivity of local sensors to bring on social transformations?

A nomadic tribe in Ethiopia, called the Afaris, believe it is a sacred responsibility to listen and share *dagu*—a word that means information, though it implies more than pure data. The Afaris are nomadic cattle herders, and they have existed for thousands of years in a harsh environment where most nomadic tribes have been wiped out. They claim that *dagu* is the secret to their longevity. "*Dagu* is life" is an Afari expression.[7]

Being nomads, Afari families travel from place to place, seeking better conditions for their cattle and themselves. Every so often they will meet another Afari family, and no matter what they are doing or where they are heading, they sit down to talk and listen, usually for hours. The exchange of *dagu* trumps all other responsibilities. They share what they have seen and heard about the environment, about health issues (both cattle and human), about political tensions, about new relationships. As they talk, they provide the facts as they have seen them or heard them, but also their interpretation of what these facts mean. They collectively make sense of the patterns that are emerging.

Children learn about *dagu* in their families and practise with their parents until they are deemed to be adept at deep listening, astute observation, and sense making or pattern recognition. Their lives depend on *dagu*. *Dagu* helps them decide when to leave an area and which area to head to next. It helps them stop the spread of disease in their cattle or families. There are severe punishments for failing to share *dagu* or for misrepresenting it. To survive, the Afaris need all their members to be sensitive and aware of emerging patterns—both natural and social. The Afaris do not believe that they can control the patterns, but that if they can understand them deeply, they can work within them and potentially nudge them or influence them.

The micro-credit movement, at its best, had elements of *dagu*. The Grameen Bank used the lending circles as an opportunity to gather accurate local information and to provide opportunities for the women members to react to changes in their circumstances. The bank relied on the lending circles to be aware of what was happening to the members who had accepted the loans, to support them when they were struggling and to mitigate the losses so there would be money for other women in the group to borrow in the future. Rather than trying to centrally control the loans, the bank institutionalized the sharing of *dagu* to improve the individual borrowers' success and to ensure the longevity and success of the bank itself. Part of the brilliance of the micro-credit movement was its recognition of normally invisible resources—the social relationships in the borrowers' communities. These relationships were critical in shaping behaviour, and creating flow.

—

The action of local sensors was also critical in Brazil's response to the HIV/AIDS crisis, and contradicted the logic that the world at large tried to force upon the situation. Key to this story is a change in perspective. A problem whose solution was deemed impossible by many was transformed by a new perspective that saw, instead, that the resources to stem the potential HIV/AIDS epidemic were readily available. Flow had been locked up by wrong assumptions and imposed definitions of what was needed, which for a brief time made it impossible to see the powerful assets that already existed in the communities.

In the early 1990s, Brazil's annual per capita income was about US$5,000, as was South Africa's.[8] Although the price of anti-retroviral drugs per patient per year was more than twice that annual per capita income at the time, Brazil refused to sacrifice its currently infected generation, and chose instead to challenge the World Bank's assumptions.

The World Bank and other observers of Brazil's pending HIV/AIDS crisis treated the problem as complicated. The complicated mode of thinking starts with the assumption that the resources and capacities of the existing system are more or less fixed and that the solution has to fit within the existing capacities of the system. Since the per capita income of Brazil was US$5,000 and the cost of the anti-retroviral regimen per person was US$12,000, the logical conclusion was that treatment of the infected was not affordable, and Brazil's only hope was to concentrate on prevention.

But when we think of the problem as complex, rather than complicated, the inquiry process unfolds in a radically different way. The starting assumption is that transformation, true novelty, is possible. The status quo needs to be understood, but it is not perceived as a constraint. Resources are assumed to consist of not only what is already part of the system, *but that which can be understood or created in relationship to each other*. Rejecting the World Bank's advice, Brazilians looked at the key relationships, the social capital, that existed in the country. Brazil's history and culture clashed with the outsiders' prognosis. From the works of Paulo Freire (*Pedagogy of the Oppressed*) and liberation theology in the Catholic Church in Brazil, the basic value of "blessed are the poor" rang loud and clear.[9] For many, at least, the idea that the poor were to be hopeless victims of a disease was intolerable. Surely there had to be a different way to see the problem?

The questions became how to provide drugs to all who needed them and how to support the existing relationships to enhance treatment compliance. This perspective echoes the notion of flow: stretching toward ideals by using the wealth of abilities at hand, total concentration and effortless productivity. We tell the story of Brazil's approach to HIV/AIDS without naming the individual leaders and players involved. The story includes over six hundred NGOs and churches as well as government, hospitals and generic drug companies. Each played a role. At some points different key players and institutions, including the federal government, were leaders and at other times they were followers. The government's brilliance was to ask questions about how things really worked across the country and to enhance the natural patterns, relationships and behaviours. This was not a top-down strategy. Nor was it entirely bottom-up. The story involved both the grassroots players and the federal-level leaders.

Deciding not to leave the poor to die, Brazil looked for ways to afford treatment, and used a controversial clause of the World Trade Organization charter that allows countries to violate patent laws in cases of national emergency.[10] Brazil argued that the HIV/AIDS epidemic was a national emergency, and insisted on the right to produce generic anti-retrovirals. It was the first country in the world to change the question and to look for a different solution—creating its own drugs. In addition, the government of Brazil gave the generic drugs to HIV/AIDS patients free of charge.

Once the treatment question was framed in terms of how to deliver help and not to whom help would be offered, a flood of activity was released across Brazil. Hospitals, clinics and public health services were well established in the main cities, but almost non-existent in rural areas. There were huge differences in the services available across the country, and in how well they reached all segments of the population. Brazil's efforts to combat the disease recognized and strengthened existing connections to enable the treatment and prevention work necessary to grapple with HIV/AIDS. Health care clinicians worked alongside NGOs and other organizations to provide the full range of services needed. They soon realized that people were more willing to come to hospitals, clinics or certain NGOs for tests if they knew they would get treatment too. The situation was not seen as hopeless. While patients were in for treatments or tests, they also received information concerning prevention. While the bulk of the spending was on treatment, the prevention goals were also being met. Rather than choosing between prevention and treatment Brazil circumvented the issue of limited resources by integrating the two.

One of the challenges of the drug treatment for HIV/AIDS is that there are many pills involved and they need to be taken at particular times of the day, some with food. Many in the North and the West assume that illiterate patients cannot comply with such a difficult drug treatment. In Brazil, nurses and other health care workers taught patients how to take the drugs, using whatever methods worked. For illiterate patients in the remote regions, they drew pictures of the sun or the moon and their position in the sky to denote different times of day. They showed pictures of food on the labels of the pill bottles to indicate those pills that needed to be consumed with food, and they helped the poorest patients link up with NGOs, churches and other organizations that offered free food. In spite of the high illiteracy rate in Brazil, the adherence rate for the drug regime was the same as in Canada or the United States.

The story of Brazil's approach to HIV/AIDS is one of recognizing the existing energy and resources in the system. By widening the definition of resources, social innovators were able to draw on an abundance invisible to others.

Complicated solutions are finite. They are clear and precise and lead to specific follow-up actions. Complex solutions lead to more questions; they continue to open up the space for inquiry and for solutions to emerge from the interactions in the system. But was Brazil's approach truly emergent? Was, in fact, the threat sensed and addressed by thousands of individual local sensors? One sign that self-organizing properties were at work in this case was the variety of local solutions that emerged. In the sophisticated urban centres, humorous and sexy advertising was used to promote prevention. In remote areas where no health care workers lived, volunteers and employees of NGOs and churches acted as health care workers by providing both prevention and treatment.

Another sign of self-organization was the pattern of unanticipated consequences. Indeed, as these local experiments took place across the country, an intense dialogue was taking place within Brazilian society concerning poverty and the large gap that existed between rich and poor. That willingness on the part of the citizenry to be involved in an open dialogue on class and wealth provided a ripe setting for public discussion of the HIV/AIDS issue. In addition, from the earliest days of the epidemic, the gay community was extremely active in denouncing discriminatory practices toward people with HIV/AIDS. That played a determining role in the government's ability to allow for the solution to emerge from the bottom up. The government was aware that for HIV/AIDS treatment to be effective, infected people needed to be given a role in the treatment of their disease; without their collaboration, the government's efforts would be wasted. The dialogue taking place at the societal level around the issue of HIV/AIDS generated a space for action and the government took advantage of this openness. The whole of Brazilian society was involved in the effort to defeat HIV/AIDS.

This brings us back to the slime mould. As we have already argued, most Western accounts attribute social transformation to the action of individuals such as charismatic leaders or social entrepreneurs. Complexity theory, Emile Durkheim and, as we will show, Jane Jacobs (profound observer of cities and societies)[11] all counsel us to look beyond the symbolic representation of the hero to the patterns of interaction that generated the energy. Social innovators tell us such energy does not flow from them; rather they find themselves swept along by the flow, just like everyone else. Ulysses Seal, whom we encountered in the last chapter, went so far as to say that unless the door seems to open effortlessly, you are not putting your energy in the right place.

In Malcolm Gladwell's book *The Tipping Point*, he showed how many social transformations mimic diseases.[12] Normal disease differs from an epidemic in the speed of spread. Unlike normal disease, epidemics move like wildfire through a community or country, or even across the globe. Flu season is a perfect case in point. Flu viruses are omnipresent, and yet for much of the year flu's spread is quite slow and usually geographically limited. But during flu season it often reaches a tipping point where the spread switches from normal to epidemic rates. There is a non-linear aspect to this—one more case of flu and the system tips to a new level.

For example, Brazil's HIV/AIDS recovery seems to have happened almost instantly in the mid-1990s, but it wasn't due to one intervention or government initiative: rather, the society reached a tipping point. More than thirty years after Freire's ground-breaking work on the poor in Brazil, his ideas were in flow in the actions taken to fight the HIV/AIDS epidemic, as each sector of society added to the solutions in ways that accelerated and magnified the spread and impact of their interventions.

So is it possible to cultivate such flow, or at least to cultivate the conditions that nurture it? Is it possible to catalyze a tipping point, or are these processes entirely out of the hands of the social innovator? Can one change the flow, or is it best to either step into the current or to stay clear?

Clearly, for flow to occur we need a common focus, some kind of feedback mechanism and a reasonable skill level. At first, the focus and the feedback mechanism may well be the property of the social innovator. Geldof, after all, came to the conclusion that "something needed to be done" and picked up the phone, initiating the first feedback to the larger system. But the skills that made Live Aid a success went far, far beyond his personal capacities. And the whole venture developed over time.

Geldof didn't have a blueprint, but an instinct. It was the energy of others that gave the instinct form and substance. But it would also be a mistake to assume that such activity would have occurred without Geldof. There is a kind of dance or oscillation between the social innovator and the collective effervescence. With flow at the individual level, we need focus, feedback and skill. But at the group level we need something more, a kind of letting go on the part of the social innovator, a kind of trust in the possibility of emergence, a faith that when critical mass is reached a tipping point will occur, and a sense that there are some simple rules for managing that emergence.

Emergence is neither good nor bad—it simply is. Henry Mintzberg, who has long written about strategy in all kinds of systems, argues that our romance with deliberate strategies has blinded us to the reality that all strategy is a pattern in a stream of actions involving both intentions and emergence. In one of his best-known articles, Mintzberg talks about the process of "crafting strategy" and organizations where strategies appear to grow like weeds in a garden: "They take root in all kinds of places, wherever people have the capacity to learn (because they are in touch with the situation) and the resources to support that capacity. These strategies become organizational when they become collective, that is when they proliferate to guide the behavior of the organization at large."[13]

Mintzberg suggests that the "deliberate" element of such strategy lies in creating broadly based goals or "umbrella strategies" on the one hand, and in creating specific "process strategies" on the other hand. These process strategies delineate patterns for interaction that stimulate strategy creation, but do not determine specific content in advance.

Such leadership is a far cry from the visionary generals of the traditional strategic-planning literature. Instead, Mintzberg invokes the idea of a potter at her wheel, someone who exercises skill, perhaps with a goal, but most critically with an ability to find and discover the opportunity in her materials. Think again of the woodcarver mentioned by Parker Palmer. He had to give up all worldly concerns in order to be able to see the bell stand in the wood. As Mintzberg notes, key to this craft is the ability to "manage patterns," to "create the climate within which a wide variety of strategies can grow," and then to detect the emerging patterns and help them take shape.

In the last forty years, Jane Jacobs demonstrated that healthy cities share a key attribute of slime moulds: cities survive and thrive best when the "pacemakers" get out of the way! Paradoxically, she was a keen proponent of urban planning and actively influenced politicians and bureaucrats. Her contention wasn't that interventions are always inappropriate. Rather, she challenged city planners to focus more on the patterns of interaction that already make neighbourhoods vibrant and self-renewing. Her keen observations of the ways neighbourhoods self-organize from a few basic rules of interaction that aggregate into a global pattern of healthy cities has been echoed in studies across the world. Over and over we have seen the failure of planned or designed communities, which frequently don't have the inherent capacity for renewal and revitalization of more organically created entities; what they miss are the rules of interaction that are inherent in naturally emerging neighbourhoods.

While Jacobs looked deeply at how neighbourhoods and cities are successful, economist Paul Krugman has studied the natural configuration of businesses and industries, and has demonstrated that most such enterprises naturally cluster with similar organizations without help from any overall designer.[14] He argues that each business is driven by local self-interest. The recurring pattern is that businesses like to have similar businesses either in very close proximity or very far away. Years after Krugman first proposed his economic models, computer games such as SimCity, which simulate economic behaviour, provide an illustration of his ideas. One can locate a series of businesses and industries across the game's landscape. However, the game then begins a series of iterations and, eventually, the landscape looks like Krugman's model—similar businesses cluster together in tight clumps, such as Silicon Valley or the garment districts in many cities, with wide spaces between clumps of the same type of business. There are some exceptions to this—local food shops or dry cleaners, for example—but usually the model holds up. The emergent patterns in these cases seem to demonstrate the necessary conditions for mutual survival.

Looking at Jane Jacobs's neighbourhoods or Paul Krugman's industrial patterns, we see that successful emergence involves building on what exists and is already working. This is known as positive feedback and is seen in a wide variety of social contexts, and even in the most social of all insects—ants. Ant colonies are quickly created by, at first, random droppings of dirt. However, one of the rules ants follow is that they are more inclined to add to a pile of existing dirt rather than start a new pile. So very quickly a few piles emerge and start to create the towers and infrastructure of the ant colony. In cities, artists cluster together, as do architects, investment bankers, tailors and actors. At times a neighbourhood can go through a very rapid transformation: one graphic designer moves onto a city block, and almost before you know it the entire block is filled with graphic designers.

What is the equivalent rule of "adding to the existing pile" for human organizations? It seems to relate to information. Ant colonies, neighbourhoods and business clusters are all very good at sharing relevant information. Ants need to know where to find food. Businesses need to know how to find trade trends, sources of labour, expertise, suppliers and current pricing information. Even in our information-rich age, physical proximity allows for a wider and deeper range of information to be shared. It is not just data businesses are looking for—data can be easily found through the Internet and other remote sources. Businesses seek to recognize the patterns in the masses of data bombarding them every day. Face-to-face interaction, accidentally bumping into each other, the sharing of gossip and the observation of emotions convey a rich array of information that helps people make sense of the patterns of business, and helps them to learn quickly and adapt to changing contexts. In other words, businesses are looking for *dagu*.

Mintzberg, Jacobs and Krugman observe what is working in the world and ask why it is working. Looking at social innovation from this perspective, we see that those who are most adept at making change recognize the local rules of interaction and then leverage them to increase their potential. When Muhammad Yunus created a change in the system to support those at the very bottom, he was recognizing such local rules. He and his graduate students found that women in their natural social circles taught each other skills and values, including honesty, hard work and support of one another when they were suffering. Yunus learned that the women had implicit codes of conduct that kept their social circles healthy.

In coming to understand such rules, successful innovations often touch universal preoccupations and concerns. Al Etmanski of PLAN talked about these universal preoccupations in his work with individuals with disabilities. "Belonging and meaning are yearnings of us all—they're universal yearnings," he says, "and if you can portray and discuss and describe and tell stories about belonging and meaning for individuals with disabilities then you find you are talking about belonging and meaning for yourself and others. It unlocks a floodgate, an awareness among all." Mary Gordon touched on the universal quality that became the title of her program: Roots of Empathy. Her anti-bullying program is now spreading throughout Canada and to other countries.

PLAN created contexts to enhance the natural rules for human belonging and creating a meaningful life. Its organizers couldn't control or predict the consequences; they trusted and worked with the emergent patterns that were created, and used these to launch their next round of learning and intervention. Gordon built a curriculum based on simple rules for empathy, bringing bullies and babies into a relationship, teaching the powerful to respond to the cues of the powerless. She knows she cannot control the outcome or how the curriculum will affect behaviour outside the classroom. Gordon, Etmanski and their colleagues first looked to understand the forces that were currently in place—what was holding the system in its status quo. When they didn't like the status quo, they implicitly knew they needed to work at the level of changing the simple patterns of relating.

—

For Paul Born and Mark Cabaj, poverty was also a human condition held in place by some very simple rules. The initiative they created, Opportunities 2000 (OP2000), set out to change those rules to transform the Waterloo region in Ontario, where they lived.[15]

For decades, the cities of Kitchener-Waterloo and Cambridge thrived with labour-intensive manufacturing. From the 1940s to the 1970s, jobs were plentiful for someone with a high school diploma. Companies making electrical appliances, rubber and plastics, and clothing, along with food processing and brewing concerns, grew and flourished, employing thousands of people. The communities enjoyed job security and were safe places to raise families, prime examples of heartland Ontario embodying the best of what we now call the "old economy."

But the old economy began to falter in the 1980s. Lured by the potential for increased profits, companies began to manufacture offshore where cheap labour dramatically reduced costs. Technological advances, particularly in the realm of labour-displacing technologies, further reduced the need for local skills. Manufacturing plants that had employed thousands began to close their doors or operate with a fraction of the previous workforce. In a single decade, twenty thousand jobs in the area were lost. And the number of families living in poverty began to rise dramatically.

By the end of the decade of plant closures, the recovery of the local economy was beginning to take hold. The "new economy" caught the imagination of many entrepreneurs in the region and, by the early 1990s, thousands of new jobs were created in the knowledge-intensive industries of computer hardware and software, telecommunications, environmental design, finance and insurance.

However, the recovery didn't stop the increase in poverty. The new reality for many in the communities was to be the "working poor." Although the country lauded the success of these communities as exemplars of the new economy, the sad reality was that by the mid-1990s, 55,000 residents were living in poverty compared to 8,300 in 1980. The success had failed many.

Voluntary-sector, charitable and church organizations responded to this crisis by increasing the numbers of food banks, shelters and recreation programs, propping up the social safety net. But this wasn't enough for Born, who worked in the community's voluntary sector and was known as a creative, insightful leader. By the early 1990s, he was beginning to seriously reconsider the role of organizations in the area that were addressing poverty. He felt the focus on alleviating poverty and helping the poor cope with their poverty no longer worked.

In 1993, Born led an organization called CODA (Community Opportunities Development Association). Through a slow and painful process, he and his colleagues hammered together a coalition and produced a successful proposal for government funding. An initiative called Opportunities Planning, it was a partnership involving more than eighteen organizations, designed to provide training to improve the quality of employment opportunities for people in the area. It also began a process of creating connections between community groups, which built social capital and made self-organization and emergence easier. After a new government was elected in Ontario in 1995, funding to support Opportunities Planning was cut. Instead of being crushed, Born seized this chance to create a new program to address the failures of Opportunities Planning.

Born worked closely with Mark Cabaj to create a new initiative called Opportunities 2000 (OP2000) in 1997 to bring together non-profit organizations, local businesses, municipal government and low-income earners to create fresh poverty-reduction strategies. Born and Cabaj were driven by the questions "How can we fundamentally reduce poverty in the region?" and "Who needs to be involved in poverty reduction in order for it to be sustainable?" They aimed to achieve a system change, not only to help individuals in need temporarily ameliorate their circumstances. Born and Cabaj set themselves the goal of getting two thousand families in the Kitchener-Waterloo area out of poverty by 2000, not by giving them help or subsidies but by building community coalitions to address the underlying structural dynamics of poverty. OP2000 helped private-sector employers understand more deeply the issues facing low-income earners. Low wages weren't the only issue; the cost of work for low-income earners could be very high, including child care and transportation. Those with health disabilities faced a difficult dilemma. If they stayed home, their incomes couldn't support their families; if they went out to work they lost their disability insurance.

Solutions needed to be found including rethinking schedules, subsidizing some costs of work, increasing basic wages and benefits, and increasing opportunities for training. Government benefits and services also needed to be restructured since some of them inadvertently penalized people for working by clawing back benefits. Non-profit organizations came to the table to see what services they needed to offer to help people move out of poverty permanently. Low-income earners themselves had a voice in these dialogues, but not as victims of the system. Like the others around the table, they were there to brainstorm, to find solutions and to look at how each sector was complicit in shaping the current context and how each could play a role to shape a more positive future. The approach was novel and successful enough to eventually earn numerous awards, including being named a UN Habitat for Best Practice in 1998 and the Imagine New Spirit of Community Partnership Award in 1999.

The initiative had a number of interesting attributes. Firstly, OP2000 maintained and even furthered the notion of partnership, pushing out to involve local corporations and municipal governments as active partners. This, Born and Cabaj felt, was key to creating system change. They developed the notion of "cornerstone institutions," which Born describes:

> We started engaging these people in the corporate sector
> because we were a fundraising organization already. We

started to understand that we needed these people if we were going to have an impact. And I'm not sure if it was even that smart; I think we just thought that if we could involve them they would probably give us more money. But, ultimately, we very quickly understood that these people had access to power that we didn't have. And I remember, within two years it was Mark [Cabaj] who said, "We've got to stop working with everybody and we've got to start focusing in on cornerstones." He called them cornerstone institutions.

To create a partnership that spanned all the private, public, and voluntary or charitable sectors, Born pushed hard to recruit more partners, even setting a quota for his people, and created working groups to support a Leadership Roundtable. In 1999 he sponsored a workshop that enabled people, many of whom were very influential leaders, with diverse interests, to come together and find common ground or their common stake in an issue. "This workshop marked the emergence of a common spiritual commitment to OP2000," says Born. "It was also the point at which a long-term strategy for poverty reduction in the Waterloo region began to emerge."

Born's approach to building participation was novel. Municipal governments and corporations in particular were accustomed to being approached to act as financial partners and, while some organizations did play this role, Born encouraged them to look first at their own operations. He pushed the Leadership Roundtable to produce an educational book entitled *Creating Opportunities: Using Human Resource Practices to Build Your Business and Your Community,* which described the great variety of things an employer could do to improve employee circumstances. Employers were encouraged to reduce poverty by "the instruments at hand: wage levels, hours of work, benefits, job reclassifications, in-house training, bursaries and so on. Of course, that first meant recognizing the implications of current employee policies and practices for the living standards of people on the shop floor."

OP2000 sought out non-governmental funds to support its operations. The organization began with a grant of $240,000 from the Royal Bank of Canada, but Born was clear that they wanted not only the money, but also all the business know-how and connections that RBC could spare. Jim Gordon, regional vice-president for RBC, was particularly attracted by this idea, as other organizations proved to be. Born said that Gordon liked the fact that "OP2000 would not be satisfied with money alone, but wanted to tap the Royal's 'heart and soul.'" Gordon committed the money and two staff secondments. "Getting involved with this initiative is probably one of the most rewarding things that some of our staff have done," Gordon said later.

Born noted that for some employers, the simple process of calculating how many of their own employees were living in poverty was such an eye opener that that information itself resulted in a gestalt shift, a sea change in attitude. One CEO took home the OP2000 material and called Born the next day to say that he hadn't been able to sleep. First thing in the morning he demanded that his human resource people look into the payroll and determine who was in fact below the poverty line. They protested, but he insisted and prevailed. Later, he raised the salary of several employees and began the process of looking more closely at how they could change the way the company worked to reduce the number of employees living in poverty. Right away, as a result of a simple exercise in salary adjustment, several families were lifted out of poverty.

As OP2000 worked hard to sign up participants, more and more organizations began to explore their own policies and practices with the

idea of innovating to reduce poverty. Ideas and initiatives and actors
flowed together. As Cabaj said, "It was a tango. I don't remember who
said what anymore. I remember us coming to the conclusion that we
would go for cornerstone leverage kind of people and organizations. Most
of them were obvious—you know, you go to the institutions that
represent powerful perspectives or sectors. We weren't really that smart.
I think it just happened—suddenly there were people [coming] to us . . .
And all of a sudden, boom. You're striking it rich."

It felt like a tipping point, a transformation mysterious even to the
organizers. It didn't feel like planned change; it felt like emergence. It
was also paradoxical—an initiative that ran contrary to the contemporary
public-policy context of tax cuts and a reduced social safety net. Yet, as
Born explains, they used the policy context of the time and the negative
energy it produced as a kind of springboard to action:

> I think the climate of cutbacks helped us, the provinces rolling
> back, the Feds cutting back. Obviously the issue of poverty was
> becoming more acute. And then all of a sudden there's
> something, there's an aggressive campaign going on and that
> attracts a whole bunch of people. Everybody was reeling from
> the budget cuts, spending all their time fighting the politicians,
> and here we were, perhaps the only voice, saying they're totally,
> totally irrelevant. We're just going to make change on our own.
> And that was so counter, and the only really positive voice out
> there, everybody just went straight to it. Everybody knew,
> including the Chamber of Commerce, that what the
> government was doing was not healthy for society.
>
> I think we were smart enough to never really know what
> we were doing, or at least not to portray it that way. We
> always had a lot of ideas and we let lots of those ideas fall and

we were a bit chameleon. So if OP2000 really [began with] a vision, I don't even remember what it was, but it was kind of intuitive and people picked up on it.

Also key to the change, says Born, was the tension created by the gap between aspiration and reality, innovation and habit. "The people who jumped up first were the *unusual* suspects in many cases. These were exactly the people we wanted to work with because the people normally doing this work, the [usual suspects], were dealing with their understandable, but ultimately ineffective, response and tended to be defensive . . . The people who joined us were extremely powerful people. It's almost like you get into a vortex. And everything, everything, everything comes along with you, and you've just got to keep going because these people are all there with you and . . . it just sort of takes you along."

This gives us an insight into the nature of leadership in emergence. Born and Cabaj perhaps set the stage and the conditions, but they were also capable of stepping back, of revealing their ignorance, of becoming, at times, followers. Born is very frank about this:

> We don't know really what we're doing. Revealing that fact, not only does it get people's defenses down, but it's a very engaging way of getting people involved in the journey. I think people sniff out pretty quickly someone who thinks they know what they're doing and they mistrust that as they know intuitively that it's impossible—it's so complex. OP2000 worked best when we were not telling anyone anything. We were just there with them. We were saying, "We're going to the same place and let's figure it out." And they know we're going to screw up, and we admit that because people acknowledge that as life. We got a lot of those people and

kept a lot of them, because of that—the humility around not really knowing what we're doing.

I guess this is leading in emergence, the tension between desire and emergence, paradox of intention and emergence. Emergence is *not* the innate desire of people. People want order very, very quickly, order in the economy, order in systems, order in whatever—order in the government. And so, the only way to [make people comfortable with] emergence is to have everyone agree that we don't know what we're doing, because if we knew what we were doing, we wouldn't be in the place that we are. And so, somehow, that enables people to go with the flow. And they don't need an answer, don't need a system, don't need a pattern. They can experiment, they can open up, they can be creative and . . . and I think that's being in the stream, it's part of it.

From 1997 to December 2000, eighty-seven OP2000 partners launched a total of forty-seven different projects that assisted nearly 1,700 people on their journey out of poverty. Clearly they didn't solve the problem of poverty for all, but they took a great step forward for many individuals and organizations. And they made improvisation a part of community response.

—

Karl Weick, a creative organizations theorist who has helped thousands of people understand both leadership and their organizations more deeply, is particularly interested in understanding the subtleties of how individuals cue each other to engage in group action—the human equivalent of the slime mould chemical signals. He has found a great source of insight in jazz music, where improvisation is king. In a great jazz concert, the unexpected is the rule. However, the ability to improvise rests on a deep-seated understanding of musical patterns *and* the ability to listen intently and respond to what fellow musicians are doing. No one and everyone leads in a jazz group.[16]

Jazz is like a conversation. When playing in a jazz band, you are responding to what was just played: you just said this on your instrument, and so I need to respond. How? What do I keep from your expression, what do we need to keep constant? What follows from that? And then the next phrase includes what stays constant but also may add a little something. What follows from that?

Finally, jazz requires not only a concentration on the conventions, the novelty unfolding, but in a group it requires intense listening, or heedfulness.[17] The conversation with self must co-exist, or at least seamlessly alternate, with the conversation with others. Jazz trumpeter Wynton Marsalis observed that in playing, as in conversation, the worst people to talk to and play with are those who, "When you're talking, they are thinking about what they are going to tell you next, instead of listening to what you're saying."[18]

So too with the social innovator. As Born and the others who experienced the OP2000 phenomenon noted, it was very much a group effort. They believed it happened through the interaction of motivated individuals who were focused on a goal, prepared to watch the patterns emerge, and who listened carefully to their own intuitions and those of others. When Born describes the experience that lay at the heart of OP2000, it sounds uncannily like a description of jazz.

The story of OP2000, as well as the others in this chapter, point to an interesting aspect of social innovation. We see here most clearly that while the social innovator is necessary for change to occur, he is insufficient by himself. A goal or focus is also necessary, though insufficient by itself. A goal helps to channel the energy but doesn't create it.

We began this chapter with the question of how momentum builds in social transformations. We realized that looking at the individuals, significant as they are to the stories, was not enough. There was something in the collective, something beyond the individual that was necessary for the birth of profound change.

When change takes hold or builds momentum toward the tipping point necessary for true transformation, there needs to be a social flow. When flow or collective effervescence occurs, the impossible truly seems possible. The social innovator cannot create this flow, but must follow the poet's advice to "let it find you." Social innovation is as much about letting go as it is about taking control. Effective social innovators know how to let it find them—how to recognize and ride social flow, trusting that the world will provide if we are open to it. And it does, time and again.

How to Let It Find You

A leader of a major philanthropic foundation might well wonder how to take these ideas to the trustees of her foundation without sounding too touchy-feely and vague. Supporting flow may feel as difficult as catching the wind. Nonetheless we would advise the philanthropist to:

• Watch for, nurture and support the conditions that generate flow and lead to tipping points.

Funders need to do much more than review proposals and write cheques for projects; they need to become part of the catalytic mix, using their considerable influence to play the critical role of bringing together people separated by traditional sector and disciplinary boundaries. In essence, funders need to help the exchange of *dagu*.

The philanthropist may wonder whether private-sector and government people should be included in this *dagu* process. Indeed, philanthropic funders are uniquely positioned to facilitate such connections. However, as with some of the ideas presented in previous chapters, the implications of complexity science for government in letting it find you challenge some fundamental traditions in the political and public policy realm. What might we say in conversation with policy makers?

- Support small, early successes to reach momentum-generating tipping points rather than relying on the blunt strategy of universal regulation.

Policy makers typically view their jobs as creating laws and regulations. In practice, this means that a great deal of effort is expended by government agencies to ensure compliance with their laws and regulations. Such an approach ignores the natural flow of innovation from early adopters through a tipping point to middle adopters, until it finally overwhelms the late adopters and resisters. An approach to regulation that views policies as safe-fail experiments instead of inviolable rules allows for emergence and facilitates flow. And what of demands for public accountability through performance measurement? From a complexity science perspective we'd offer the idea of information targets.

- Set information targets, not just performance targets.

Information targets are indicator points that, when reached, tell you to pause and look again at what's going on. A gasoline gauge on an automobile provides an example of an information target. When the gauge shows a quarter full, you don't say to yourself, "Good for me, I've succeeded in using three-quarters of a tank of gas." Instead you think about how much farther you can go on the amount remaining.

OP2000's vision of raising two thousand people out of poverty by 2000 was a useful goal for attracting and motivating people. But such a clear goal can also become a liability if policy makers or funders fixate on it as a measure of success. For evaluation purposes multiple information targets are helpful. Who is coming to the Roundtable? Who is absent and why? What is each player learning about her own workplace? What changes has each player (employers, government, charities and employees) made to reduce poverty? What lessons are the players learning? How are they sharing them? Again, such an approach, like the other developmental evaluation techniques we have mentioned, supports both emergence and innovation.

—

What are the implications of letting it find you for voluntary- or non-profit sector practitioners? What advice can we offer the agency director of a small non-profit organization?

• The flow can find you only if you're in the stream. Get in the stream and learn to observe the currents around you.

Running a voluntary-sector organization is typically all-consuming. There is never enough staff, resources or time. Everyone is stretched to the limit. Under such circumstances it's easy to become isolated and self-absorbed, and focus all your attention on the organization's functioning. Connecting with others, building collaborations, scanning one's environment with colleagues and sharing information all feel like luxuries, valued, to be sure, but easily put off until things are under control and today's crisis is past. But things never quite get under control, and there's always a new crisis. Just as isolated slime moulds will forever remain solitary, isolated service providers are destined to become encumbered by a fortress mentality, enveloped in a fear of the world's larger, uncontrolled and uncontrollable forces. In contrast, interacting slime moulds gradually come together into a greater whole. *Dagu* connects people, but depends on those who travel, circulate, collect and share information. That's the information stream. For the flow to find you, you have to be in that stream and develop the capacity to read the current and detect the patterns. Then, like a skilled kayaker navigating tricky currents, you can make your work and the work of your organization part of the flow.

• Don't just gather information, share it.

In the competitive environment of the voluntary sector, where agencies often compete for funds, it's easy to become an information hoarder rather than a knowledge sharer. In the successful ant colony, each ant adds to the dirt pile. Add your dirt—your information—to the existing pile. It's through your contribution to the pile that others can find you and come to value you. Remember, *dagu* is about sharing information, not hoarding it.[19]

—

We would like once again to end this chapter by speaking to people, particularly young people, who are trying to figure out where and how they can make a difference. What do we have to say to them about letting it find you?

- Think of social innovation as a craft to be learned through experience and apprenticeship. Start where you are, immerse yourself in social innovation and find social innovators from whom you can learn this craft.

The notion of craft discussed in this chapter is an idea seldom heard in modern parlance. Part of what we are attempting to portray in this book is a set of craft-like skills and mindsets that we have found to be common among effective social innovators. These include pattern recognition, which is especially critical to letting it find you (so that you can recognize it when it finds you), strategic big-picture thinking (so you know where you are in the grander scheme of things), and knowing how to interpret information and convert it to knowledge you can use to move forward. Craft evokes skill, dedication, engagement, mastery, knowledge born of experience and practice, and a feeling of intimacy and harmony with the materials at hand; in this case those materials are the patterns and elements of social innovation.

- You are not alone.

If you have a good idea, and you believe that the world needs this idea, then trust your instinct. While no one else may be doing it yet, it is likely that many people are also feeling this call to action. Bob Geldof picked up the phone and just started talking. So can you. Begin by sharing your idea with everyone and anyone. When others are excited, invite them to join in. Don't try to control the energy, just encourage the conversations and let the momentum build. The energy of others is your most important resource. Keep the goals front and centre—let the means emerge. Have patience, and keep talking. *Dagu* is life.

Suddenly I saw the cold and rook-delighting Heaven
That seemed as though ice burned and was but more ice,
And thereupon imagination and heart were driven
So wild that every casual thought of that and this
Vanished, and left but memories, that should be out of season
With the hot blood of youth, of love crossed long ago;
And I took all the blame out of all sense and reason,
Until I cried and trembled and rocked to and fro,
Riddled with light. Ah! When the ghost begins to quicken,
Confusion of the death-bed over, is it sent
Out naked on the roads, as the books say, and stricken
By the injustice of the skies for punishment?

W. B. Yeats, "The Cold Heaven"

6. Cold Heaven

One of the challenges in social innovation is knowing when we have succeeded and when we have failed. When can the ideas and actions of a few truly be said to be a social innovation? If a particular initiative reduces the murder rate in a community for ten years, and then murders rise again, was the initiative a success? If a breakthrough in community-based science restores a lake that is later destroyed by acid rain, was the initial rescue a failure? If smallpox seems to have been eradicated and then re-emerges, was the earlier alleged triumph a sham, or can it be paradoxically true that smallpox both was and was not eradicated?

Those who struggle to make a difference have to face two paradoxes. The first is that success is not a fixed address. The second is that failure can open the way to success.

Those who dare to attack seemingly intractable problems and those who fund such initiatives are motivated by glimpses of a better world. If you count yourself among such dreamers, you know what it feels like to feed on the possibility of a world transformed. The price of failure can be steep: loss of ideals, loss of hope, sometimes even harm to those you sought to help. And harm to yourself. Social innovation is clearly high risk. It can become what Yeats referred to as "cold heaven." And yet it is a risk we need to take if we are to remain compassionate, adaptive, resilient and experimenting.

If any man has experienced cold heaven in our times, it is surely LGen Roméo Dallaire, who, as witness to the Rwanda genocide, was "stricken / By the injustice of the skies." The experience left him shaken to the depths of his being, and haunted by memories "that should be out of season."[1] His story is a cautionary tale on the effects of harsh judgments, the most brutal of which we often inflict on ourselves. Failure becomes more than the failure of an idea or its implementation; it becomes personal failure.

Dallaire headed the small UN peacekeeping force in Rwanda. He witnessed unspeakable horrors as extremist Hutus massacred over 800,000 Tutsis and moderate Hutus in the space of a hundred days in the late spring and summer of 1994. He and his peacekeepers had advance evidence of the plans for a genocide, and he had sought authority to seize Hutu arms caches, but his superiors at the UN had instructed him to alert the local authorities and take no action himself to disarm the militias. Then, as bodies filled the streets and rivers, the general tried in vain to attract the world's attention to what was going on. In an assessment that military experts now accept as realistic, Dallaire argued that with five thousand well-equipped soldiers and a free hand to fight Hutu power, he could bring the genocide to a rapid halt. Again, the UN turned him down, constrained by the domestic and international politics of its Security Council members. He asked the United States to block the Hutu radio transmissions that were provoking and guiding the massacre. The Clinton administration refused to do even that.

Instead, following the deaths of ten Belgian peacekeepers assigned to protect the president of Rwanda, Dallaire's forces were cut to five hundred men, as one of the most horrific genocides in history unfolded. Dallaire, frustrated and disheartened by the passive attitude of world leaders, repeatedly confronted his superiors—to no avail. The international community occupied itself with arguing about the definition of genocide, placing blame elsewhere and finding reasons not to intervene.

Some blamed Dallaire for the tragedy. In Europe his "failure" became front-page news. The Belgian Senate, hurting over the loss of its soldiers, branded him "careless and unprofessional."[2] Though Dallaire and his unarmed peacekeepers managed to save the lives of thirty thousand Rwandans, in Dallaire's eyes this was not enough. He returned to Canada haunted by the ghosts of the murdered, who had become his constant companions on the roads of Rwanda. Repeatedly, he contemplated taking his own life as a solution to his disgrace, shame and guilt. He knew cold heaven in every molecule of his body as he "cried and trembled and rocked to and fro." Understanding finally that he was suffering the effects of post-traumatic stress disorder, he entered psychiatric treatment, courageously going public with his diagnosis, a rare act for a general. But in July 2000 he was found drunk in the park across from his apartment building in Hull, Quebec, a once proud and distinguished man, a public servant and peacekeeper, whose life had been shattered. His medical retirement from the Canadian Forces soon followed.

Though Dallaire continues to fight the demons of doubt and guilt, he has re-entered public life to tell the story of Rwanda for the world community and all who will listen. When Dallaire gives speeches, as he often does these days, he emphasizes our common humanity and our shared responsibility to protect the innocents of the world wherever they may be. In his keynote address to a major international conference in Toronto in 2005 (where the Canadian Evaluation Society and the American Evaluation Association jointly awarded him the Presidents' Prize for Speaking Truth to Power), he said that he still awakens in the night to cries of wounded children and the inconsolable weeping of survivors. He told of his utter helplessness as he listened while a man seeking his help died at the other end of the phone line. Every day he runs the risk of being suddenly hijacked by sense memories of the stench of rotting bodies and the sight of hacked-off limbs stacked by the roadside.

And he still feels deeply and personally responsible. Clearly hoping to console him, one young woman at the conference stood to tell him that he had done as much as anyone could have done under the circumstances. Without a moment's hesitation, he replied, "When you're in command, you are in command. That's how it is. I was in command. 800,000 died. The mission I had responsibility for turned into catastrophe and I was in command. I failed to convince my superiors and the international community to take action. I didn't have sufficient skill or influence. When you're in command, you are in command. That's how it is. I was in command."[3]

—

Many whose efforts at social change have failed are haunted by endless and unanswerable questions: What if I had slept less, tried harder, spoken louder, risked more? What if? What if? What if? This is how the failure of an effort involving many different people and forces becomes personal failure.

There is a devastating scene at the end of Steven Spielberg's movie
Schindler's List, when the Jewish factory workers Schindler has saved
gather to thank him as he is about to flee the liberating armies. Instead
of experiencing their gratitude as a blessing, Schindler falls apart,
weeping and whispering to his friend, "What if I had sold my wedding
ring. I could have saved two more. I kept my car . . . that could have
saved more." One of the most difficult aspects of social innovation is
that it is never enough, that there is always so much more to do. The
result can be a sense of deep isolation and even despair.

Paul Born shared with us his own experience of cold heaven:

> [There were times when] we felt alone and abandoned. It
> didn't matter, all the good things that had happened, that
> were happening—everything seemed like it was unravelling.
> At such moments, it's much deeper than isolation, it's
> despair. I know people in this work, social innovators, and, in
> private, quietly, we talk about this to each other. I recently
> had a meeting with a person who created the largest network
> of business leadership in the country and I asked him, "When
> is the last time someone said to you, 'Well done!'? When's the
> last time someone said to you, 'You're a national treasure.'
> When's the last time?"
>
> And he said, "No one has ever said that to me."
>
> And I know, both in this person's personal life and in his
> work life, that he reached the depths of despair, went from the
> highest to the lowest. He had to deal with that. Out of that
> came this massive re-emergence. It took about two and half
> years in which he came up with an incredible renewal of what
> was to be the whole next pattern in his personal life and work.
> I think there are aspects of going in and out of that dark place

for all of us. Somewhere, if you're going to talk about all of social innovation, somewhere you have to deal with despair.

I know someone who follows what's happening among charitable organizations like most business people follow the stock market. He recently told me that he had become concerned about people he had not heard from for a while. He tracked them down and found out that in one year two had committed suicide and others had burnt out and just dropped out.

A lot of attention is given to getting social innovation started. That's what I call the challenge of turning on the light switch. But that switch doesn't just get turned on and then stays on. The switch goes on and off, right? That's our challenge—not just getting the switch to turn on, but getting it to come back on when it goes off. Inspiration and purpose are not necessarily strong enough to keep it on all the time.

When I wanted to start Tamarack[4]—I don't know if I should say or talk about this on tape but . . . , yes, I'm comfortable doing that, it actually doesn't hurt anymore—I had as close to a nervous breakdown as I've ever had in my life. I spent six months in therapy. And that whole time, I didn't want the switch to go back on. I was fighting it because I knew what turning it back on would mean. I had been there. That switch had been on in me once too often as far as I was concerned. I needed now to be selfish for myself and for my family. I didn't want to have to live with the consequences of the switch going on again. I worked with the therapist and I think she helped me put a dimmer switch in. And so, I know now it's not off or on. I can put it up to full volume or I can turn it down.

Do you remember the book of Job? It's one of the great stories. Other than *King Lear*, I know of no other story that helps you understand the depth of despair—despair that almost reaches insanity. Yet, as he laments his woes, he finds some solace. That's how it is sometimes.[5]

A sense of inadequacy, a sense of hopelessness, of chronic disaster, of despair: Born mentions the story of Job, upon whom hard times fall. Job's friends became demon evaluators who pointed out to him that such ills wouldn't have befallen him if he hadn't fallen short, sinned in some elemental fashion. When the stakes are high—lives lost in Rwanda, children dying, poverty, starvation and misery—the guilt can be overwhelming. "And I took all the blame out of all sense and reason / Until I cried and trembled and rocked to and fro / Riddled with light."

How does the social innovator regain perspective? Born talks about the therapist who helped him install his dimmer switch. Just as Job was chastised by God for the pride that made Job think he was responsible for the patterns of creation, Born argues, social innovators must simultaneously keep their head in the stars and their feet on the earth. Think about Ulysses Seal and the scientists in the Conservation Breeding Specialist Group, who continue to work tirelessly while knowing with certainty that they will fail, ultimately, to save all the species they love. One CBSG member explained it like this: "I do not believe for a moment that we are going to win. I do not openly say this . . . but it is not going to happen. I continue to work because, even if the desired result is not forthcoming, I have still done my duty . . . I have done whatever I could to bring it about, regardless of anything. This is important to me spiritually."[6] He copes by setting boundaries around his own efforts, asserting that a certain animal will not disappear "on my watch." That watch will last his lifetime, but by thinking about his mission in this way, he makes it human-scaled—manageable enough to carry without succumbing to despair.

Social innovators will inevitably face skeptics, critics, naysayers, disbelievers, dissenters and the possibility of failure, perhaps even the likelihood of failure. Fierce conviction is required to sustain innovation through various internal and external struggles, and to be an agent for change requires bold thinking and grand vision. Complexity theory shows that great changes can emerge from small actions, that the possible, even the "impossible," can happen. That's the part that involves keeping your head in the stars. But what about keeping your feet on the ground? How do social innovators do that?

They face reality.

Reality testing has a bad reputation among some visionaries. Leaders tend to attract and surround themselves with believers—true believers, positive thinkers, hope-springs-eternalists. Criticism is well known to undermine creativity, which is why it's outlawed in brainstorming exercises. But how can social innovators fully engage both their critical and creative faculties? The answer lies in a commitment to reality testing that is no less fierce than the commitment to reach for the stars.

Jim Collins, author of the best-selling management book *Good to Great*, studied with his research team how good companies become great.[7] Not many companies actually made the grade, but those that did all had leaders who lived the paradox between absolute dedication to a great vision and ruthless commitment to staring reality in the face. Collins called this the Stockdale paradox in honour of James Stockdale, the fabled American navy officer who survived years of torture in North Vietnamese prisons. Stockdale had an unwavering belief that he would survive and an equally unrelenting vigilance about the realities of his captivity. He was constantly attuned to what was happening to him and his fellow prisoners, and adapted his survival strategies and tactics accordingly, day by day. When, after a short period of unusual good treatment, he realized that he was about to be used as propaganda to show the world how well prisoners were being cared for, he brutalized his own face so that he could not be so used. Hearing how Stockdale managed to stay ever hopeful and survive, Collins asked him how he would characterize those who didn't make it, those who died in captivity. That's easy, Stockdale replied. The people who died were the unwavering optimists, the ones who said they'd be out by Christmas, and then by Easter, and then by summer's end, and then again by Christmas, always and only focusing on some future hope. They died, he said, of broken hearts.

The great companies Collins's team studied all shared an unrelenting belief in a better future *and* an obsession with data about the realities of the present. They monitored the results of their initiatives relentlessly, tracking what was working and not working, and how their environment was changing. They allowed themselves no rose-coloured glasses, no blind spots, no positive thinking. *Ruthless attention to reality was the common path to attaining their visions.*

The businesses and multinational companies that Collins studied are ultimately judged by the bottom lines of market share and profit. The reality testing available for social innovators is called developmental evaluation, which is grounded in complexity science.

Undergoing traditional forms of bottom-line evaluation is a cold heaven experience for many social innovators, because following the money is such a limiting way to judge success in this sphere. Yet resources are often scarce for those who fund and support social innovations, and they want to know whether their funds have been well spent to achieve desired goals. Funders ask whether it's right to risk supporting initiatives that are as yet unproven. Social innovators offer visions and dreams. Funders and the evaluators they often hire want concrete, clear, specific and measurable goals. They also want to know step by step, in advance, how the goals will be attained,[8] an approach doomed to failure in the complex and rapidly changing world in which social innovators attempt to work. Developmental evaluation, in contrast, involves tracking the effects of efforts as they unfold and adapting to what is learned. Evaluation helps chart a changing path of innovation by providing rapid feedback. Let's look at an example.

In 1977 three Roman Catholic nuns started St. Joseph's House in the inner city of Minneapolis, inspired by Dorothy Day's philosophy of "comforting the afflicted and afflicting the comfortable."[9] The sisters took their passion public and persuaded individuals and churches all over the metropolitan area to support building a women's shelter in one of the poorest areas of the city. Over the years dozens of volunteers answered the call, helping hundreds of women and children find safety in a welcoming environment of support. However, as important as the temporary shelter was for the many poor women and their children who found solace there, it was little more than a Band-Aid.

By the early 1990s even that small success was threatened as the area surrounding St. Joe's became the centre of a crack cocaine epidemic: drug dealers had claimed the streets and landlords had abandoned many buildings. One long-time activist, Char Madigan, tells of their effort to shame the dealers: "First we got posters that said, 'Up with hope and down with dope,' and we'd march up and down the street, and the dealers would march with us and they've got their own poster, 'Up with dope and down with hope.'"[10]

St. Joe's guests and nearby families began to keep their children inside as drug dealers and prostitutes did their business out of neighbourhood buildings that had fallen derelict and police regularly ran by with guns drawn. At the north end of the block, where two major Minneapolis streets intersected, once-thriving small businesses (a gas station and a grocery store) were abandoned.

This was the situation faced by community activists Deanna Foster and Mary Keefe when they took over the leadership of St. Joe's and renamed it Hope Community in 1997 as a symbol of their vision. They decided to attempt a housing revitalization project and began by trying to talk with local residents. But the residents wouldn't even come out on the doorsteps for conversations, so afraid were they of the local drug dealers.

The Hope Community began confronting this reality on its own turf. Foster and Keefe built a playground at their centre and renovated a duplex that shared a driveway with the largest drug house. They fenced the yard, and then the porch, because the drug dealers would run across the porch to get around the fences in the yard. As the pair later wrote, "The drug house was a triplex, with several small children there who were terribly neglected and abused. The children were so desperate for something to do that they would climb onto the garage or climb over the fence, anything to try to reach our playground. The playground system had a crawl tube on the ground that was five or six feet long. We cut a hole in the fence and put the tube through it to give the little kids their own doorway into our place. The drug dealers would have to embarrass themselves to crawl through the tube, and some did. The kids' private door powerfully expressed the idea that drug dealers are not welcome here, but children are always welcome."[11]

Then one day Foster and Keefe decided that the only way to get rid of the dealers altogether was to buy the drug house, even though it felt like they were paying ransom. Nonetheless they called several of their donors, raised the money and bought the house. Then they tore it down and built a new duplex on the spot.

Buying the drug house was not part of some strategic plan. It was a reaction to what they faced every day. But after successfully ridding the community of one major drug house, Foster, Keefe, and other community residents and leaders came together to shape a new vision of a Children's Village in the area, which would include housing for hundreds of poor families from diverse backgrounds, a place where children would be safe and nurtured and valued. Then they sought support for their vision from philanthropic donors, sending out letters and proposals.

Keefe and Foster remember vividly what happened next: "One day a handwritten check for $500,000 arrived in the mail! We put it in the bank and lost sleep: How are we going to be good stewards of this gift? This serious investment called our bluff. We had a big plan, and suddenly someone believed in it and backed up that belief in a big way. We had to refine our own understanding of how we were going to shape our future. It's one thing to have an idea; it's another thing to be responsible for actually nurturing that idea and bringing it forward in a responsible way."[12]

When flow begins, it brings both terror and delight, sleepless nights and energetic days. Foster, Keefe and community residents had created a vision for a major community revitalization effort centred around the somewhat vague idea of a Children's Village, an economically and socially vibrant place where families from diverse backgrounds could congregate safely as neighbours and friends. They found many believers, but the vagueness and grandeur of the vision also brought out the skeptics. Foster says she and Keefe struggled to keep their focus: "We never promised to build the whole thing. Children's Village was a vision. But it shocked people. It really shocked people. Some were pleasantly shocked and then said, 'Well, that was fun,' and went on their way. Others were critical, saying we were unrealistic. Suddenly we were out there in the public eye, and we didn't know how Children's Village was going to happen. We only knew it would."[13]

They faced the criticism by finding the flow in the community, facing the daunting reality of what might lie ahead, and working day to day— acting, getting feedback, learning, acting, in a cycle of emergence. In their own words: "We almost had to do it, not backwards, but in alternate order. Normally, when an organization gets half a million dollars, they have spent a lot of time in a more linear process, thinking through what they are going to do. What is the goal? What is the work plan? What will it cost? Who is the staff? You get the community input, all that stuff, and then have this whopping proposal, right? But it didn't happen that way at all. It was, 'Here's the vision, here's the money, now, make it happen.'"[14]

They had to figure out what to do as they tried things, paying close attention to how people reacted, and adapting to what they saw and heard. They weren't following a carefully laid out plan, but where day-by-day success and failure took them:

> One of the criticisms we get is that we don't have a linear, goal-directed approach. We don't assume where we are going. We ask: Who's here? What are people experiencing? What are they believing and hoping? What is their understanding of

community? And what is our understanding of all the things we've done? We keep trying things, building understanding and building community around ourselves. We are about uncovering, discovering, and creating. The process is natural. It grows organically.

But it's more complex than that too, because at the same time there's strategic thinking going on. We also have to ask: Where is the land out there? Where's the money? What are the opportunities? Where are the potential partners? What are the potential pitfalls? How could all this fit together? What would happen if we did this?[15]

This is a perfect example of what we call developmental evaluation. The questions that Foster and Keefe were asking themselves differ radically from those asked in most evaluations, which often begin and end with

a fixation on whether goals were attained.[16] Such evaluations make accountability their primary purpose. In contrast, developmental evaluation makes learning primary. Here are Foster and Keefe again:

We may try things that don't necessarily succeed on their own but end up teaching us something and creating other opportunities. We bought a house and ended up selling it a short time later, but we recouped our money, learned about the block the house was on, and from that house came one of our best tenant leaders. Another lesson came when we were smaller. We tried having our own construction company, learning quickly about the limits of that strategy and acting accordingly. . .

Intuition is important, but intuition isn't just a random thought. It grows out of strategic, integrated thinking. We operate in a huge matrix of reality. We don't focus on

relationships with people in the neighbourhood but also on the
real estate developers, the people buying and selling real estate,
and yes, often ripping people off. We immersed ourselves in
that community because we had to—it was going to have a
big impact on our neighbourhood. We have to deal with the
city departments and a multitude of other public agencies.
We immersed ourselves in the whole picture and learned
from it so we could strategically respond to opportunities.[17]

Foster and Keefe understood reality as messy, not orderly; emergent,
not controlled. They understood social innovation as an ongoing process
of experimentation, learning and adaptation. They worked from a
complexity perspective, seeing and engaging the connections between
the micro and macro. They monitored the big picture, the whole picture:
national housing, community development and real estate patterns;
interest rates and international finance; government policies,

philanthropic funding trends and priorities; research on community
revitalization. They grounded new efforts in knowledge of the history of
the community, a history they learned from talking in-depth with those
who had been around before them. At the same time, they were fully
enmeshed in the day-to-day reality of working in the community,
interacting with local government inspectors, city planners, social service
agencies, local businesses, local funders, and, because it was part of the
community's reality, drug dealers, prostitutes, and the police. In the
summer of 2004 the Hope Community celebrated the opening of
Children's Village Center, which houses Hope's headquarters and
community centre, as well as ninety new units of affordable housing.
A couple hundred more are in development.

Such social innovators epitomize the Stockdale paradox. They are
fiercely visionary and hopeful even while determinedly grounding their

actions in the cold heaven of daily reality testing. For them, hell is not failing; hell is delusion. Hell is kidding yourself about what's going on, for therein are the seeds of failure sown. In its essence, developmental evaluation is about learning what works, acknowledging what doesn't work and learning to tell the difference—with none of the blaming of cold heaven attached.

—

The Hope Community story is about two unusually astute and effective social innovators inventing as they go along, and helping to bring a whole community with them. But more established organizations can apply the ideas of developmental evaluation more formally to help them adapt to a changing environment.

Duluth is a port city in northern Minnesota, at the westernmost point of the north shore of Lake Superior. It is home to about 85,000 people. In the early 1980s Duluth's economy was hit hard by mine closings, a regional farm crisis, declining shipping activity, the phasing out of the local air force base and even a Jeno's Pizza plant pulling out. The area's unemployment rate rose to 15 percent. In 1982, a community-based poverty-alleviation program called the Damiano Center was founded as a temporary response to this crisis.[18] Looking for a name that would resonate with people of many faiths, the founders of the organization drew inspiration from the Church of San Damiano in Assisi, birthplace of Francis, the saint renowned for his work with the poor. The Damiano Center began as a soup kitchen in the cafeteria of the former Sacred Heart Catholic School, a hundred-year-old dark-red brick building on a steep hill overlooking downtown Duluth and the Lake Superior harbour.

When the unemployment crisis ended, the Damiano Center did not. An ecumenical organization supported by dozens of churches, donors and volunteers, it still feeds an average of two hundred people a day, 15 percent more than in 1983, in a city with a population that is virtually unchanged. And, gradually, the Damiano Center has grown into more than a soup kitchen. It added a clothing exchange that gives out forty thousand items of donated clothing a year. Its "Clothes That Work" program offers good clothing to those who need to look presentable for job interviews and at work. It also provides advocacy services and referrals to people in crisis.

In 1998 the organization began the Opportunities Cooking program: twelve weeks of free training in cooking and food sanitation for hard-to-employ adults. The community kitchens model from Washington, D.C.,[19] provided inspiration and a place to start, but the founders tweaked the model to fit the smaller size and specific needs of Duluth. The goal

was to establish a food service program to train and graduate twenty people and assist them with employment. In the first year fourteen people graduated, 60 percent of whom were still employed a year later. This is an average result for programs of this kind. In the second year, the Damiano Center began efforts to move people beyond entry-level positions and introduced the concept of career development, but the outcomes changed very little for three years. Jean Gornick, the executive director at the time, reflects: "In hindsight, Damiano's early efforts at training people for employment were incredibly naive. So much so, that today I am surprised we experienced even the limited degree of success we did."

Gornick wanted something better than merely average results, so she tried doing some formal developmental evaluation to figure out what needed to change. She says, "We were making program decisions based on assumptions rather than facts, and so we did some evaluation and used the findings to make several changes that greatly improved outcomes for our students."

The first breakthrough came when they recognized that they needed to focus beyond graduation (and a higher graduation rate) to getting students employed and helping them stay employed. Taking a careful look at the program, Gornick found that staff was spending more than a month a year celebrating graduation (planning, inviting, cooking and decorating). Instead, she decided, "We retained the celebrations, recognizing their importance to people, but scaled them way back. The lead staff person began to spend more time bringing good employers to the table and instituting incentives for work retention. An example of this is the three-month bonus to graduates if they remained employed. Mentors and support groups, as well as staff support, are now provided post-graduation."

The Damiano Centre also found that the organization had fallen into a complicated intake procedure that, in some cases, had actually become a barrier to getting needy people into the program. Staff simplified intake, converting to a bottom-line screening of math and reading levels, cognitive functioning and readily identifiable mental health issues. They introduced a three-week orientation period with a contract for the session signed the first day of week four. They set up an ongoing process for getting feedback from students, including conducting focus groups with staff and students at the end of each twelve-week session. The result of these changes is a 98 percent placement rate in employment and a work retention rate of 70 percent after one year on the job.

Interviews with independent leaders and funders in Duluth confirmed
that the centre had come to be regarded as an effective and respected
organization that was making an incremental but important difference in
the community. However, even as it attained a high level of success, the
environment in which it operated was changing. Partly because of its
success, the Damiano Center underwent a successful labour unionizing
effort aimed at non-profit organizations, even though it only had sixteen
full-time and seven part-time staff. Then the economic recession in
2001–02 hit Duluth hard. Funding for programs dried up. New
government regulations threatened some established operating
procedures, including eligibility and screening requirements. The
hundred-year-old building needed major renovation.

Gornick identified these trends early. She knew better than to let the
program's past successes crystallize into a formula. In an uncertain
environment mired in political controversy about the future of
employment and social service programs, the program adapted by using
dagu. Staff built new collaborations, sought new funding partners and
explored new opportunities, such as expanding from cooking to catering.
They showed funders how they were applying what they were learning
from evaluation and framed these changes as developments, not just
improvements, a key difference in perspective. Gornick says, "At each
stage we did the best we could with what we knew and the resources we
had. Now we're at a different place in our development—doing and
thinking different things. That's development. That's change. That's
more than just making a few improvements."

—

The current political environment is awash with calls for accountability;
politicians have discovered that ranting about inadequate accountability

makes good sound bites, and philanthropic funders emphasize their commitment to good stewardship by highlighting their commitment to accountability. In both the political and philanthropic arenas, this has led to more paperwork and reporting requirements, but not particularly meaningful accountability. Why? Because it's like a game of charades in which programs guess at what will satisfy the demand for accountability without actually internalizing what it means to be accountable. Organizational leaders and program managers concentrate on demands to satisfy external authorities and funders.

But for value-driven social innovators the highest form of accountability is internal. Are we being true to our vision? Are we dealing with reality? Are we connecting the dots between the here-and-now and our vision? Are we walking the talk? And how do we know if we're not? What's different? What's emerging? These become internalized questions, asked ferociously, continuously, because the effective social innovator wants to know.

That doesn't mean that it's easy to ask such questions and face the answers. It takes courage to look at whether you are on the right path, and even more to face whether you are deluding yourself about the possibility of real change. Within such insistent inquiry lurks despair, the shadow side of social innovation. In "The Cold Heaven," Yeats grappled with his own sense of the mistakes and missed opportunities in his life— his accountability to himself. Developmental evaluation, first and foremost, should help you live inside the Stockdale paradox, reaffirming faith in your getting-to-maybe vision even as you adapt tenaciously to day-to-day realities.[20]

How to Survive Cold Heaven

What wisdom can be extracted for philanthropic funders from a cold heaven perspective on complexity and social innovation? First, we'd emphasize that support for social innovation involves more than financial support.

• Support social innovators psychologically and socially, as well as financially.

Funders rightfully expect those they fund to be grateful, and they are grateful, but funders should likewise be grateful to those willing to work on the front lines of social transformation. Funders often talk about the risks they're taking with their funds, not seeming to fully register the risks social innovators take in putting their careers and often their lives on the line. The sacrifices, the psychological stresses, the doubts, the burnout, the dark nights of despair—who should be grateful to whom? Social innovators desperately need financial support, but they also need psychological and social support.

• Support reflective practice among social innovators.

The isolation of some social innovators can contribute to their cold heaven doubts and despair: they lose perspective, they feel abandoned. They can be so driven by the urgency of the tasks at hand that they treat reflection as a luxury. However, bringing social innovators together to systematically and analytically reflect on what they have learned and to rigorously identify patterns of effective action is not a navel-gazing luxury. It is the hard work of standing still.

—

Harvesting the insights of social innovators can build knowledge about social innovation and effective philanthropy. But there are barriers embedded in traditional philanthropic practice to overcome. Many philanthropic funders say they value learning and want to know what works and doesn't work, then, in the next sentence, they reaffirm their bottom-line thinking about accountability: "You (and we) will ultimately be judged by whether you attain your goals and achieve results." This tension between learning and accountability is seldom recognized, much less openly discussed. *Accountability messages trump learning messages every time.* As surely as night follows day, this attitude leads those who receive funds to exaggerate results and hide failures—the antithesis of genuine reality testing and shared learning. Funders need to engage in their own thoughtful reality testing about the messages they're sending and the incentives (and disincentives) they're providing to learning. If a philanthropist asked us how to approach the evaluation of social innovation, we'd suggest the following:

- Support learning as a meaningful outcome—and reporting on learning as a form of authentic accountability.

That can work for private philanthropy, and we've seen it work. But can it work in the public sector? Politicians run on promises of achieving results, not fostering learning. Imagine a candidate for public office saying, "We live in a complex world and I would certainly not presume to predict what results my policies would achieve. If elected I plan to set some things in motion, see what happens, learn, adapt accordingly and see what happens next." Yet our "cold heaven," complexity-inspired advice to public servants is precisely this:

- Create and nurture experimentation and learning about social change, especially failed policies and initiatives.

It is idealistic and naive, perhaps, to suggest this, but surely it's a better approach than the usual knee-jerk response to things that go wrong in the political realm, which is immediately seeking someone to blame. Consider how failure is approached among venture capitalists and product innovators. New ventures, new businesses and new products fail at very high rates; indeed, successes, especially great successes, are rare. No one seems particularly surprised by this, and it certainly doesn't stop people from trying new things. Yet in the public sector, proposals are created and evaluated with the expectation that every one of them will be a great success—that anything short of completely solving a problem is a failure. Creating a civic culture in which people understand that things seldom work as expected, especially when trying to solve complex, intractable problems, would support a shift toward learning. This shift is not to avoid accountability but rather to make learning a focus of meaningful accountability.[21]

• Support small "safe-fail" initiatives to learn what works and doesn't work before implementing policy changes widely.

The notion of "safe-fail" emphasizes trying things out in a limited way, with lots of feedback and monitoring to learn what happens when an intervention is introduced. It is *safer* to have a policy fail while it is in an experimental pilot stage than when it has been widely adopted and is being broadly implemented. Having government support safe-fail experiments amounts to creating a public-sector research and development capacity. This could be a small but important part of a ministry's total budget. Just as money managers recommend that investors construct a diversified portfolio with only a small percentage of assets in the category of high-risk/high-return venture capital, likewise we're suggesting that public funds be used to support experimentation within society by allocating a small but meaningful portion of revenues to social innovation.

—

Let's imagine, now, that some courageous and far-sighted policy makers actually followed this advice and invested a slice of public funds in learning-oriented, complexity-inspired, safe-fail social experiments. How should voluntary-sector organizations respond to such opportunities? What can our director of a non-profit agency do?

• Embrace meaningful and ongoing reality testing; make serious developmental evaluation part of the organizational culture.

Many voluntary-sector organizations and social innovators seem to let the difficulties of measurement become a rationale for avoiding data altogether. Others let the inevitable ambiguities in data become a reason not to struggle with interpretation. Still others say they intend to start doing evaluation but never quite find the time or resources, along the way becoming quite adept evaluation procrastinators. Enough with the excuses. Evaluate.

• Report, discuss and learn from failures as well as successes—and keep these balanced and in perspective.

Fear of failure—or perhaps, more accurately, fear of less than complete success—creates a barrier to acknowledging what's not working, sharing that understanding with others, and learning from each other as a community of innovators. It's natural to attempt to avoid criticism and judgment by keeping your own counsel and hiding from those who would force a confrontation with cold reality. In contrast, the leaders of the Hope Community engaged with critics and skeptics and used those encounters to examine their assumptions, test their progress and reaffirm their vision.

The danger in acknowledging failure is taking on too much personal responsibility. So to social innovators and social change practitioners we commend this lesson from "cold heaven":

• Avoid taking more personal responsibility for failure (or success) than is appropriate.

Social innovation and transformation are the products of many forces. Overly harsh self-criticism and self-blame hinder rather than enhance learning. Ironically, taking too little personal responsibility is just as big a problem as taking too much. Blaming others and explaining away failures due to larger forces can hinder learning every bit as much as becoming mired in self-doubt and existential angst.

Complexity science offers a perspective beyond simple personal responsibility. Studies of systems change show that things often get worse before they get better. The dismantling of the old system before the new system is ascendant can feel—and can be—the coldest of cold heavens. Not only are things not getting better, they're getting worse. Shallow allies flee, criticism intensifies, vision flounders, reality crushes. The antidote to despair is to embrace reality testing as a cold slap of water that awakens the senses to a new day and renewed commitment. This is how the leaders of the Hope Community avoided despair in the face of seemingly overwhelming negativity, initial community apathy and early failures.

—

For people trying to figure out where and how they can make a difference, we would highlight the courage and commitment of the people whose stories we've shared. We believe they would say to you, as we do:

• Don't let fear of failure hold you back. Be prepared for ups and downs, and live the Stockdale paradox: eyes on the stars, feet on the ground.

Using Yeats's soul-wrenching encounter with a "cold and rook-delighting heaven," we opened this chapter with the story of Roméo Dallaire's breakdown over his inability to stop the Rwandan genocide. It is only fitting that we update that story. Having faced the ultimate question of his own culpability, he has re-emerged from the depths of despair to engage actively in efforts to prevent such devastating lapses by the international community. Speaking, writing, organizing and collaborating as a private citizen, he has joined the ranks of social change agents working to make a difference to world peace and justice. His book, *Shake Hands with the Devil: The Failure of Humanity in Rwanda,* has been critically and popularly acclaimed, winning the Governor General's Literary Award for Non-Fiction in 2004 and the 2004 Canadian Booksellers Association Author of the Year Award and Award for Best Non-Fiction Book. The documentary film *Shake Hands with the Devil: The Journey of Roméo Dallaire* won the Audience Award at the Sundance Film Festival in 2005. Dallaire received the United Nations Association in Canada's Pearson Peace Medal from Canada's governor general and has been appointed to the Canadian Senate. In all this, he still speaks and acts out of a profound sense of his "responsibility to protect." In his speeches he urges young people to engage because each person can make a difference. He has travelled to Africa to testify at the trials of the Rwandan genocidaire at the United Nations International Criminal Tribunal for Rwanda. As this is being written he is active in the effort to get international action to stop the killing in Darfur, Sudan.[22]

Dallaire's story reminds us that our individual efforts at bringing about change inevitably intersect with larger societal, political, economic, social and global forces. We cannot control these forces, but we can understand them and adapt our efforts as we learn through every twist and turn. Ultimately, we each have to find our own pathway through the conflicting messages:

You always act alone.	Your actions are always connected to and interacting with the actions of others.
Individuals cannot make a difference because they are mere parts in a larger, dynamic system.	Small actions can lead to large changes even the small actions of one individual can tip a system toward change.
If you make a mistake, you can cause great damage.	Where you stumble, there your treasure is. The only lasting failure is the failure to learn—and failure to apply that learning going forward.
It's crazy to be hopeful in the face of inhumane human realities, stricken by the "injustice of the skies."	It's crazy not to be hopeful in the light of real stories, such as Dallaire's, of transformation and engagement, facing and surviving "cold heaven."

Human beings suffer,
They torture one another,
They get hurt and get hard.
No poem or play or song
Can fully right a wrong
Inflicted and endured.

The innocent in gaols
Beat on their bars together.
A hunger-striker's father
Stands in the graveyard dumb.
The police widow in veils
Faints at the funeral home.

History says, don't hope
On this side of the grave.
But then, once in a lifetime
The longed-for tidal wave
Of justice can rise up,
And hope and history rhyme.

So hope for a great sea-change
On the far side of revenge.
Believe that a further shore
Is reachable from here.
Believe in miracle
And cures and healing wells.

Call miracle, self-healing:
The utter, self-revealing
Double-take of feeling.
If there's fire on the mountain
Or lightning and storm
And a god speaks from the sky

That means someone is hearing
The outcry and the birth-cry
Of new life at its term.

Seamus Heaney, "Doubletake"

7. When Hope and History Rhyme

The maybe in *Getting to Maybe* includes wondering whether hope and history will rhyme. As Seamus Heaney observes, when new life is at its term, in that moment when hope and history rhyme, the social innovator may experience a juxtaposition of despair and possibility, of outcry and birth cry, of beginnings and endings. In fact this experience, we argue, defines success in social innovation.

We've followed the ups, downs, overs and arounds of social innovators, watching with them for tipping points and struggling to understand what it all means. Time and again, we were drawn to the questions intrinsic to the very idea of social transformation: What happens over time? Can and should the successful social innovation be sustained? If social innovation is not a fixed address, how can we ever say we have arrived? When hope and history rhyme, what happens to those who have devoted themselves to fostering change? How, we wondered, does the social innovator endure success?

Just when things seem to be going well, social innovators often encounter their greatest obstacle: success. When a small initiative suddenly tips into a huge success, those involved face new challenges. For Bob Geldof, success meant being catapulted into a highly political arena in which he faced constant scrutiny. For Paul Born, success meant making an effort to roll out his formula to multiple communities across Canada—no small task. For Mary Gordon, success has meant finding the right training going forward to ensure proper replication of her programs. For Jeff Brown it meant developing a ten-point program that could be taken to other cities, and a deep, deliberate standing still to understand the essence of what had allowed him and his group to succeed in Boston, at least for awhile. For some, success can be as disorientating as facing failure. Indeed, more so, because these leaders are prepared, even determined, to fight on in the face of failure, but what does one do in the face of success? The story of Candy Lightner offers insight into what can happen when hope and history rhyme.

In 1980 Candy Lightner's twelve-year-old daughter, Cari, was killed by a drunk driver—a repeat offender. Brought to trial, the driver was reprimanded and released. At the time, Lightner was a real estate agent in Sacramento, California. In her 1990 memoir, *Giving Sorrow Words,* she wrote: "I promised myself on the day of Cari's death that I would fight to make this needless homicide count for something positive in the years ahead."[1]

Lightner was certainly not the first mother to be outraged about lenient drunk-driving laws that returned chronic drunks to the streets. Even in 1980, when her daughter was killed, the statistics were well known and widely publicized. Drunk driving was the major cause of traffic fatalities in North America. In fact, it remains the single largest criminal cause of death in Canada, where approximately 1,500 people are killed each year as a result of impaired driving, a number about three times higher than the country's murder rate. The situation is worse in the United States.

Following her daughter's death, Lightner founded Mothers Against Drunk Driving (MADD). During the eight years she headed MADD, she built the organization from a one-woman crusade into a worldwide movement. She began by writing to newspapers, appearing on radio and television shows, giving speeches, seeking out other mothers whose children had been killed by drunk drivers and organizing demonstrations. She formed a network of survivors of alcohol-related crashes to campaign for victims' rights, engage in legislative advocacy, form grassroots organizations and call attention to the contributions that women and children can make in bringing about meaningful and substantial social change.

The goal of MADD was to reduce drunk-driving traffic fatalities, and the proportion of traffic fatalities that are alcohol related has dropped 40 percent over the last quarter-century. Most observers give substantial credit for that decline to the efforts of MADD. When, in 1993, the U.S. Fatality Analysis Reporting System statistics revealed that alcohol-related traffic deaths had dropped the previous year to a thirty-year low, the federal National Highway Traffic Safety Administration credited MADD along with tougher laws. The organization has also been highly effective in raising public disapproval of drunk driving. As early as 1984 results from a Gallup survey on drunk driving showed the public becoming increasingly less tolerant of drunk drivers and more supportive of stiffer penalties. That trend was an early indicator of MADD's growing influence and success.

MADD works through its chapters in all fifty states and ten Canadian provinces, and its many international affiliates. While drunk-driving fatalities have declined, MADD believes they remain unacceptably high, and so the organization continues its campaign to educate, prevent, deter and punish. It has caused judicial reforms throughout the United States. MADD helps victims, monitors the courts and works to pass stronger anti-drunk-driving legislation. With a worldwide reputation for vision and effective action, today's MADD enjoys unprecedented success as a charitable organization. What began with anger and a broken heart has developed into an association of more than six hundred chapters and two million members and supporters, with net assets of US$23.5 million. Since its start in 1980, more than 2,300 anti-drunk-driving laws have been passed.[2] In a 1994 study by the *Chronicle of Philanthropy*, MADD was the most popular non-profit cause in the United States, ranked second among the most strongly supported charities and third on the most credible list.[3] People continue to contact the organization to request guidance in establishing their own grassroots organization.

Surely, this is a success, one that many would attribute to Lightner herself—her determination, passion and organizing skills. She indeed forged a mission of hope. But "her" success grew within the social context of her efforts. On multiple fronts, history was unfolding to rhyme with her personal crusade.

The year in which Lightner's daughter was killed, 1980, was the year in which Ronald Reagan was elected president of the United States. His campaign, and that of the Republican Party generally, included a national call to get tough on crime, stop drug use and make judges take criminals off the streets. Reagan had just completed two terms as governor of California, where MADD would be born. His campaign rhetoric indicted the court system, especially "liberal" judges, for lenient sentences. Thus began a quarter-century of legal and judicial reform, which still continues, to "toughen" the courts. Such efforts include mandatory sentencing guidelines, and longer and harsher sentences, especially for repeat offenders. These larger efforts paralleled perfectly the specific MADD agenda. In 1982, in time for the congressional elections, Reagan announced a presidential task force on drunk driving and invited MADD to serve on it. That same year MADD backed a resolution enacted into law by Congress to establish the first National Drunk and Drugged Driving Awareness Week, and the federal "21" minimum drinking age bill was enacted.

Then Nancy Reagan launched the anti-drug "Just Say No" campaign. The school program DARE (Drug Abuse Resistance Education) was founded in 1983 in Los Angeles to fight all kinds of drug use, and played a lead role in defining alcohol as a drug. MADD and DARE rode parallel and mutually reinforcing waves, as DARE became adopted in nearly 80 percent of U.S. school districts, involving twenty-six million students, and in more than fifty-four countries around the world.

In the wake of civil rights marches, feminist protests and anti-war demonstrations in the 1960s, police had come to be viewed by the youth culture as the enemy. But both MADD and DARE built their strategies for change on enlisting the police as partners. The police were early supporters of MADD's efforts to toughen drunk-driving laws and increase enforcement. Police were the teachers in the DARE program. These efforts emerged at a time when instead of just arresting criminals, police were working to rebuild their community connections by engaging in crime prevention, enlisting community support, reaching out to youth, and undertaking community policing initiatives. The agendas of the police, MADD and DARE overlapped and reinforced each other.

In the 1960s, many social ills were considered the result of poor family backgrounds, inadequate education and insufficient social support systems, and the response was symbolized by the liberal "Great Society" programs of the time. Alcoholism became widely understood to be a disease rather than simply a sign of character weakness. Programs for the treatment of alcoholism and drug abuse flourished along with treatment programs for juvenile delinquents, child abusers, sex offenders and others who had come to be seen as victims of society's past injustices and lack of caring. The "Just Say No" campaign marked a turning point toward the current emphasis on personal responsibility. Reagan's huge tax cuts especially targeted treatment programs, most of which were considered by the 1980s to have failed to achieve their promises of redeeming the fallen. Punishment replaced treatment as the order of the day. Prison populations grew exponentially and changed their missions— not rehabilitation anymore, but keeping criminals locked up as long as possible. MADD's underlying messages of vengeance and punishment, especially for repeat offenders, resonated deeply with the backlash against coddling criminals, drunks, addicts, child molesters and rapists. The cultural tide had turned from hopeful rehabilitation to harsh condemnation, from treatment to punishment.

Another way in which MADD's success rhymed with history was that it was a female-led movement at a time when feminism was ascendant. MADD culminated a century-long process of ever-increasing female activism and social innovation. The earlier temperance movement in the United States, like the suffrage campaign, had been led by women. By the 1980s the role of women in society had changed so fundamentally that MADD activists faced none of the barriers their earlier temperance-crusading sisters had faced. While MADD has male members and allies, MADD was born as and remains a female-led movement, benefiting from the sea change in women's role in society that epitomizes the twentieth century.

Historically, drunkenness was portrayed in movies and television as amusing. Drunks did and said funny things. Moreover, drinking was perceived as a coming-of-age rite—and right. It was one of the ways that boys became men. Men drank, and drank to excess, simply a fact of life. Changing these deeply embedded cultural perceptions and expectations would require major social innovation. MADD's first innovation was making such changed expectations part of its explicit agenda.

In 1986 MADD launched its first telemarketing programs to spur growth in grassroots support and serve as a major public awareness campaign to educate the general public on drunk-driving issues. That same year Project Red Ribbon was introduced, and one million red ribbons were distributed as motorists pledged to drive safe and sober during the Christmas and New Year holidays. In 1987 a national toll-free hotline was created to provide victim support. These strategies and developments coincided with increasing public interest marketing, using advertising to promote positive messages for social change.

It has been said that nothing is so powerful as an idea whose time has come. It is clear that the time was right for Lightner's initiative. The fledgling organization that she founded took wing on currents that bore it upward. But she herself did not continue to soar with it. *Along the way, MADD lost Candy Lightner.*

Eight years after she had founded it, she left the organization in a widely publicized display of anger. She left because MADD changed its goals, becoming far more prohibitionist than she wanted or supported. "I didn't start MADD to deal with alcohol," she said. "I started MADD to deal with the issue of drunk driving."[4] She believed that if MADD really wanted to save lives, it would focus on ways to stop the real problem drivers. Her departure spawned false, yet tenacious, rumours that she had been arrested for drunk driving.

Some charge that MADD has, indeed, become a prohibitionist organization. In the early years of MADD's greatest policy successes, drunk driving became defined in the United States as driving at the .10 blood alcohol content (BAC) level. That is now being redefined to .08. At least five states have attempted to lower the blood alcohol limit to .05.[5] Doris Aiken, the founder of MADD's sister organization, Remove Intoxicated Drivers (RID), wants to lower the level to .04. Recalling the tragedies of September 11, the RID leader insists that "drunken drivers are the terrorists of the road." There is now a move in Vermont to define drunk driving at the .02 BAC level. What's the ultimate goal? Tina Pasco, MADD's local director in Santa Monica, California, asserts that "the only safe amount when you are mixing drinking and driving is zero—double zero. No alcohol."[6]

Those who oppose this prohibitionist focus, including Candy Lightner, argue that it is misguided and ultimately ineffective. No one should drive after drinking, they argue, but "zero tolerance" is counterproductive, impractical and a waste of limited resources.[7] They assert that most alcohol-related traffic deaths occur when other important causal factors are present, such as using a cell phone, fatigue, drug use, inexperience in driving, road rage, speeding, poorly lit roads and failure to use safety belts.[8] And, of course, most traffic fatalities don't involve any alcohol at all. If MADD really wanted to reduce traffic fatalities, they argue, it would also care about these other major causes of traffic deaths. MADD is no longer a safety-promotion organization, they complain, but an anti-alcohol organization.

These charges are but one example of the antagonism MADD's success has spawned. A web search will turn up anti-MADD sites attacking the organization for greed, corruption, lack of integrity, opportunism, using junk science, lies, selling out, overpaid staff, unscrupulous fundraising tactics, mission drift, a too-narrow mission and so on. Thus do successful social innovators find themselves in a never-ending battle with supporters and opponents about what their mission is and ought to be, and how they ought to operate. From the rush of enthusiasm, from finding flow, the leader is suddenly outside, unwelcome and sometimes anathema, attacked by former allies.

Is Candy Lightner's story characteristic of many "successful" social innovators?

Certainly, when we hear the phrase "the perils of success," we often think of Icarus, who flew too close to the sun and melted his wings. Or we may think of the old saw that "power corrupts" and wonder whether successful social innovators suffer from hubris. Was Lightner a victim of her own success? Or has MADD itself been seduced by success to reach too far?

Nothing turns success into tragedy more certainly than the prideful blinders and arrogance of hubris. Success can create resistance to ongoing change, incapacity to adapt to that change and undervaluing continuing innovation to build on past successes. Both individual leaders and entire organizations are vulnerable to hubris. Consider the cautionary tale of the NASA space shuttle tragedies.

When *Columbia* crashed on February 1, 2003, killing all seven astronauts aboard, a thirteen-member board of inquiry undertook a comprehensive independent investigation. The direct mechanical problem that caused the crash was damage from a foam tile that came loose during liftoff, but the more basic cause, investigators concluded, was NASA's own culture. Since the 1986 *Challenger* disaster, which also killed seven astronauts, a culture of complacency had crept into being at NASA—including the tendency to define a potential safety problem as insignificant so as not to require a fix that would cause delay. In its 248-page report, issued in August 2003, the *Columbia* board of inquiry concluded that the space agency lacked "effective checks and balances, does not have an independent safety program and has not demonstrated the characteristics of a learning organization . . . The board strongly believes that if these persistent, systemic flaws are not resolved, the scene is set for another accident."[9]

Harold Gehman, a retired admiral who served as the board's chairman, told reporters at a Washington briefing that NASA tends to follow safety procedures diligently at first, then will "morph or migrate away" from that diligence as time goes on.[10] In addition to detailing the technical factors behind *Columbia*'s breakup, just minutes before its scheduled landing at the end of a sixteen-day science mission, the board's report laid out the cultural factors behind NASA's failings. It said NASA mission managers fell into the habit of accepting as normal some flaws in the shuttle system and tended to ignore, not recognize or not want to hear about such problems even though they might foreshadow catastrophe. "These repeating patterns mean that flawed practices embedded in NASA's organizational system continued for years and made substantial contributions to both accidents," the report said.

During *Columbia*'s last mission, NASA managers missed opportunities to evaluate possible damage to the craft's heat shield from a strike on the left wing by flying foam insulation. Such insulation strikes had occurred on previous missions, and the NASA managers had come to view them as an acceptable abnormality that posed no safety risk. Spy-satellite photos of *Columbia* might have identified the extent of damage to the shuttle, but NASA managers didn't take the opportunity to pursue them. But most of all, the report noted, there was "ineffective leadership" that "failed to fulfill the implicit contract to do whatever is possible to ensure the safety of the crew." Management techniques in NASA, the report said, discouraged dissenting views on safety issues and ultimately created "blind spots" about the risk to the space shuttle of the foam insulation impact. The report noted: "Little by little, NASA was accepting more and more risk in order to stay on schedule." Also: "The program was operating too close to too many margins."

The NASA story is one of technological rather than social innovation, but there are nonetheless some parallels to be drawn. As Ulysses Seal noted when he was asked why he seldom seemed elated by the awards that he won, "When a person is good at getting things done, or at helping others to do them, he or she can come to think they are responsible for what happens. And they're not. Whether the outcome is good or bad, it is hubris to accept too much blame or praise."

Hubris is ultimately what led to the *Columbia* disaster—a kind of rigidity that no social innovation can afford. Successful innovators need to become skilled at asking probing questions about their own successes. They may need to find a modern version of the Roman servant assigned to stand behind triumphant generals as they entered Rome to the adulation of the masses, whispering continuously in the general's ear: "All glory is fleeting."

Consider our health care system. Medicine in the past century has made huge advances. Illnesses and ailments that were a death sentence a generation or two ago now are more often than not curable or controlled chronic conditions. These great successes in medicine have reinforced patterns of behaviour whereby the doctor or the health care provider is the expert and the patient is a mere recipient of the services. Does this constitute arrogance or a form of hubris?

In the United States today, as well as in other Western countries, some hospitals are taking the brave stance of making "patient-centred care" more than rhetoric. If patients truly are at the centre, then the information asymmetry traditional in health care is invalid. Patients should have access to information not only to inform their own care but also to shape the providers, institutions and policies that affect them; there is a growing movement in the United States for hospitals to voluntarily report their performance results for comparison with industry standards. A patient in a truly patient-centred philosophy should not be thought of as a cost or a mere recipient of services but as a significant resource and a true partner in care.

What does this mean specifically? Dr. Don Berwick can explain better than we can. He is a clinical professor of pediatrics and health care policy at Harvard Medical School, a practising pediatrician at Boston's Children's Hospital, and a consultant in pediatrics at Massachusetts General Hospital. He is also the president and CEO of the Institute for Healthcare Improvement, whose mission is to radically improve health care effectiveness.[11] He gives a vivid depiction of how patients are typically treated in hospitals by telling the story of Bert, an innovative and highly skilled lawn mower racer, who developed techniques to induce riding mowers go over sixty-two miles an hour even though they are manufactured to go no faster than about five miles per hour. Here is how Bert is treated in a hospital, as told by Berwick:

> Put Bert in a Johnnie, so his underwear shows. Label his arm. Talk at his bedside as if he weren't there. Put it in Latin. Tell him the visiting rules. He takes his own pills at home; but not here. Instead, take his pills away, and then use your own in a little paper cup and dole them out to him four times a day. If he asks for his laboratory result, tell him you need permission

to show it to him, because the numbers might scare him—
the numbers might scare the 13th fastest lawn mower rider in
America. Yell out, "Bert," in the waiting room, but introduce
yourself as "Dr. Jones," or not at all. Keep him waiting. Keep
him guessing. Make him tell you his name, address, and
phone number five times; make him tell his symptoms ten
times; take his blood pressure twenty times without ever
telling him what it means. Hurt him with an error, but never
tell him, because he might be angry.

Make noise. Lots of noise. 24–7. Wake him three times a
night, and at 6 a.m. rounds. Clang the cart, beep the beepers,
laugh in the corridor. Feed him, but not according to his
nature. When he asks for a snack at night, tell him the
kitchen is locked, or bring him a slice of white bread. Make
the smells strange, the lights harsh, the bed mechanical, the
night lonely, the day boring. Do not ask Bert for his opinion,
or his help, or his preferences, or his values, or even his
knowledge of himself.

In short, tell Bert, regarding the lifetime and skills and
wisdom and special knowledge and dexterity and friends and
neighbors that he brings to us, tell him, "No thanks, Bert.
No thanks. We'll take over."

Bert can make a lawn tractor go 62 miles an hour. Can
you? Well, no. But what does that have to do with anything?

Everything. Patients bring us wealth, and we make it slag.
Patient-centeredness means valuing everything—
everything—that the patient, the family, and the community
bring into the struggle against disease—the struggle for
health. It means using the natural capital of natural healing.
We are not authentically patient-centered until we have
wasted none of it.[12]

Don Berwick is trying to lead a social transformation. From the perspective of the status quo and those with power, his work is highly subversive in that he is asking health care providers to live up to the rhetoric about patient-centred care that they espouse but rarely follow. He is also challenging the hubris of modern medicine and medical practitioners, many of whom have come to believe that they, alone, are responsible for the health of their patients.

Perhaps Candy Lightner's departure from MADD had nothing to do with hubris. Perhaps, like Don Berwick, it was Lightner's subversive insistence that her focus was on stopping innocent deaths. Perhaps the hubris was on MADD's side. Certainly, Lightner's commitment became intertwined with other streams of social momentum. In that sense, her personal crisis must also be viewed in the context of larger societal forces. To understand this, we introduce another concept from complexity science: fitness landscapes.

"Fitness landscape" is a term coined by complexity scientist Stuart Kauffman, who argues that neither the external (the larger system) nor the internal (the individual agent) tells the whole story of how social innovation evolves.[13] Instead, he says, we need to think about evolution more as movement on a rugged landscape that shifts as we try to move across it—a fitness landscape.[14] If our goal is to climb the highest summit and we find ourselves on a landscape with flat plains with one huge dominant peak, the goal is clear—climb the mountain.

But a landscape becomes more rugged—with more peaks and valleys— as more factors come into play. Picture the Rocky Mountains, which look more like a series of peaks and valleys with no dominant peak in sight. If our goal is climbing the highest summit, how do we figure that out? We can see only the nearby peaks. We may believe we're climbing the highest mountain only to find yet another range lies beyond with even higher peaks.

Now add another level of complexity—that the landscape evolves as we move across it—and we have a more accurate image of the challenges of social innovation. Not only do we face a rugged landscape where we may not be able to see beyond our current location, but the peaks themselves are shifting as a consequence of our actions and the actions of others. A mountain may become a hill or even a valley over time, and vice versa. Consider the process of raising a child. While child-rearing manuals abound, parents still struggle to get it "right." For no sooner do they think that they have found the formula than the child changes and they have to find a new approach. Add more children, each changing and affecting siblings, and all affected by the parents, and you have the perfect picture of a continuously shifting "fitness landscape."

If we view MADD's story as one of a co-evolving, shifting landscape influenced by and influencing external forces, Lightner's eventual departure makes more sense. Even as MADD was shaping societal attitudes and public policies on drinking and driving in Canada and the United States, it was shaped by those changing attitudes and policies. When Lightner started her crusade to reduce drunk-driving fatalities, the goal was clear, and she and her cohorts became more and more skilled at navigating the landscape they encountered. MADD's timing coincided with a variety of societal and political trends that meant that the spread of its ideas was rapid and profound. The time was right, the mood of the community was right and there were enough powerful experiences and stories of loss and grief that they attracted tremendous support.

However, as momentum grew, the landscape shifted and the peak (goal) of reducing drunk driving began to seem less significant than the neighbouring peak of zero tolerance. The movement for zero tolerance gained ground in part due to the efforts of MADD. Lightner may have been caught off guard by the powerful internal and external shifts that led MADD's focus to move to zero tolerance. It is very difficult to see the shifting landscape when all your energies are focused on climbing the current mountain. Even as we get close to maybe, social innovators must not forget to stand still, to encounter the powerful stranger and to stay close to flow. As with Candy Lightner, sometimes such re-assessment can lead social innovators to feel that, if they are to stay true to their calling and determination to get to maybe, the best course is to leave the very organization they have created and move on to new challenges. This is facing a cold-heaven decision.

Remember Jeff Brown? He and his colleagues in Boston made tremendous progress: the peak seemed to be in sight as the murder rate plummeted from 150 per year to 40. They learned a great deal and shared their learning by creating the TenPoint Coalition movement. However, the landscape was shifting even as they experienced success. As local gangs lost their grip on the neighbourhoods, international gangs saw an opportunity to move into what they perceived as fertile territory. The youth murder rate began to increase for the first time in five years. Brown realized the mountain they had climbed was shrinking as another large mountain erupted before them. They needed to regroup and begin the ascent up a different mountain, a landscape with new challenges and opportunities. They, like Paul Born, wanted to scale up their approach and spread it to other communities, other cities. And this posed new and different challenges.

Brown's and Lightner's stories are powerful reminders of how ephemeral success can be. But viewed from a fitness landscape perspective, setbacks are not failures but rather the inevitable and expected aspects of a co-evolving world. Indeed, one might say that as an innovation is successful, it redefines the landscape in which it has emerged, assuring that its immediate success is short-lived even as the foundation has been laid to take on new challenges. Social innovators find themselves, at the moment of success, standing still and redefining how to get to a new maybe.

—

Having arrived at an approach that was in great demand across the country, Al Etmanski, Vickie Cammack and other members of PLAN might have bathed for a moment or two in a sense of accomplishment. Instead, by 1997 a sense of malaise and even of failure seemed to hover around the edges. Progress in replicating the PLAN model was frustratingly slow, and what progress did occur was strangely unsatisfying. New chapters seemed to take a very long time to become independent. A sense of isolation began to grow, even a sense of despair. Yet the sense of responsibility was stronger than ever. Reflecting on this, Etmanski said, "We did not want our work to be seen as another interesting experiment that goes nowhere, except for a few hundreds or thousands of people. We were experiencing, my wife and I, feelings of guilt, of worry, of frustration."

C.S. Holling and his colleagues who developed the adaptive cycle model distinguish three kinds of change: (1) the abrupt, spasmodic learning that characterized the initiative and exploration that created PLAN; (2) the incremental or adaptive learning that characterized its start-up and growth to maturity, when PLAN was working out the details of the organization, its philosophy and its approach to relationship building; and (3) most importantly for our book, transformational learning, generally characterized by relatively sudden "breakthroughs," when multiple systems or scales align in a cascade of novelty. Let us look more closely at this idea of scales and cascades, for it can be critically useful in helping social innovators assess the potential for hope and history rhyming.

Scale in ecological systems is a key component of resilience. From the small scale of pine needles, to the larger scale of trees, to the life and death of whole forests, systems existing at different scales do not evolve and cycle in the same time frame. Likewise, in social systems, individuals, groups, organizations and institutions (such as economies, cultural systems and legal systems) go through the adaptive cycle at different rhythms. Much deep novelty or transformation, therefore, comes from "cross-scale" or cross-system interactions, which is what Holling terms "panarchy," after Pan, the Greek god of chaos and play.[15]

Under certain circumstances, novelty at lower levels can create a revolt at higher levels, pushing the broader system into release. When a forest is healthy, with sufficient variety, a pest such as the spruce budworm will have a local and limited impact. However, if the forest lacks variety, and is homogeneous and overconnected (without the patchy variation of a healthy forest), the tiny spruce budworm can destroy the mighty forest rapidly. Similarly, when a political regime has become brittle and unresponsive, ideas that have been simmering among smaller groups of individuals may suddenly be taken up by the general public to create an overthrow of an old order, a transformation that is often highly unexpected. For example, few people anticipated the destruction of the Berlin Wall and the unravelling of the Soviet Union that followed. For decades there had been resistance, but it had been ineffectual. Yet when the first group of Berliners took up their hammers and began to destroy the wall, no one stopped them. Those in power did not marshal a response. Instead, in a classic example of "cascade," one regime after another in the Soviet bloc crumbled and fell.

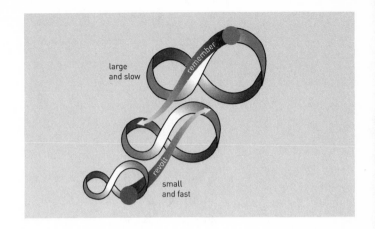

Cross-scale interactions can operate in an opposite fashion as well. Individuals in an organization, for example, may try to introduce a new program or service to clients, only to find that the rules of the broader system demand that the new service be made to resemble the old as much as possible. Holling and his group refer to this as "remembrance," the way in which laws or cultural norms will limit and control new ideas or projects. As any inventor knows, most ideas die on the drawing board. When we use the phrase "the time is right," we are talking about cross-scale or cross-system conditions that allow an innovation to flourish, when at another time it would have no chance of doing so.

So when Etmanski and Cammack felt guilt, worry and frustration at the slow spread of PLAN, they were describing what many social innovators we talked to experienced. Each success only increases the pressure to scale up, to find the tipping point where the innovation becomes the longed-for tidal wave of change that was, after all, their dream. In another paradox of social innovation, this time of success is also a time of standing still and re-evaluating what it means to succeed. Scaling up is rarely a linear process that involves doing more of the same, like producing another cake by using the same recipe. Etmanski and Cammack recognized that spending their time travelling across the country to nurture fledging PLAN organizations was not only exhausting and time consuming, but also ineffective in creating the hoped-for transformation. They felt they were losing their edge: they were no longer really engaging the powerful stranger, the forces that render people with disabilities marginal and define "a good life" in ways that exclude them. They decided to stop focusing on replication across the country and instead move to trying to create the conditions for a tipping point. This meant turning their attention to the policy level, to go directly to trying to change the underlying structures, or in Holling's language, the "slow variables" that exclude people with disabilities.

Etmanski puts their realization this way:

> At the heart of most projects of dissemination, is this belief that if you share the model, that by itself is sufficient to create a critical mass . . . [But] we believe that the insights, the inventions associated with our work are so profound that we have a responsibility to embed those in the structures of our society, if you will, to make them part of the water supply, or the air we breathe, diffuse them into statutes, funding priorities and the like. When one looks at the challenge in that perspective, one begins to think very differently about one's responsibility than when one is thinking about just making it available to families in other parts of the country. There is an implicit assumption that if you create a critical mass, that will contribute to the regulatory changes . . . and that's not the case.

Etmanski and Cammack recognized that, at bottom, their work was about citizenship: What is citizenship based on? What does it mean? How can we reconstruct our definitions of citizenship to acknowledge the rights and responsibilities of all of us? The reach of these questions extended to not only people with disabilities but also anyone who was marginalized in some way—the homeless, people with addictions, minorities.

So Etmanski and Cammack began again. While maintaining a close involvement with PLAN, they brought in a new executive team to help them run it so they could create a sister organization, Philia, aimed at effecting policy reform for people with disabilities.[17] They organized dialogues and invited thought leaders in Canada such as authors Mark Kingwell, Michael Ignatieff and John Ralston Saul to these dialogues. Etmanski and Cammack's own measure of success was to follow the post-dialogue speeches and writings of their guests looking for their reflections on disabilities. Etmanski and Cammack sought partnerships with national media, particularly the National Film Board, to tell their story to a broader public. They also increased their efforts to directly influence policy makers, building relationships with politicians at local, provincial and federal levels and lobbying for such changes as allowing families of people with disabilities to shelter savings for the future care of their family members who were disabled. Etmanski and Cammack were trying to change the deep structures—the culture of ideas, the laws and the flow of resources. Only by influencing this larger context, they felt, could they create the conditions for PLAN to flourish across the country.

So success, as we have said repeatedly, is not a fixed address; we don't arrive there. We may pause there, standing still to reflect on our next move. But if the goal is social transformation, the next step is rarely obvious. It often means working on multiple fronts and paying attention to readying the system to respond to the innovation, as much as trying to duplicate the innovation. Edwin Land, inventor of the Polaroid camera, whom we described as someone who knew how to let ideas flow, also knew that the invention of a new product was only half the equation. Launching a successful product did not mean simply replicating it many times. Instead, it meant supporting the product launch by managing context. He called this the "second great invention":

> The second great invention for supporting the first invention is finding how to relate the invention itself to the public. It is the public's role to resist. All of us have a miscellany of ideas, most of which are not consequential. It is the duty of the inventor to build a new gestalt for the old one in the framework of society. And when he does, his invention calmly and equitably becomes part of everyday life and no one can understand why it wasn't always there.[18]

Successful social innovators seem to understand intuitively about working across scales, managing the context in which the successful innovation will seem not radical, but as normal as the air we breathe.

Ulysses Seal described how he deliberately tried to organize in different ways at different levels in order to induce change across systems. He paid particular attention to moving from local to regional to international action, all the while attending to the particular traits of each level while organizing across levels. He said:

> We're trying to organize now geographically. We're trying to organize taxonomically. We're trying to organize in terms of professional knowledge and skills. All three at once. It is a mangle tangle. The evolution of it and how it's happening is partly driven by classical hierarchal logic. It's driven by the sheer complexity of the problems that we're dealing with as

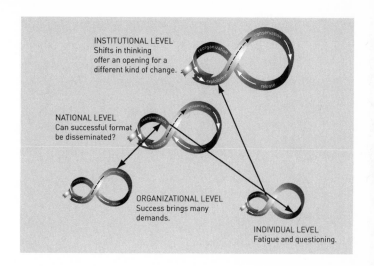

INSTITUTIONAL LEVEL
Shifts in thinking
offer an opening for a
different kind of change.

NATIONAL LEVEL
Can successful format
be disseminated?

ORGANIZATIONAL LEVEL
Success brings many
demands.

INDIVIDUAL LEVEL
Fatigue and questioning.

Cross-scale interactions [19]

we try, experimentally, to cope with them. The problems,
when they were first stated ten years ago, were widely agreed
to be impossible. What we're doing is saying that they can't
be impossible.

The "mangle/tangle" Seal described requires ongoing adaptation to what
emerges. The process is ever dynamic.

Muhammad Yunus concluded his autobiography by reflecting on the
many offshoots of the Grameen Bank that now exist around the world.
One such progeny was Calmeadow, founded in Canada in 1987.[20] The
idea was to bring the concepts of Grameen Bank to the poor in Canada,
an example of "scaling up." However, shortly after Calmeadow started
operating, large commercial banks entered the market of loans to the
poor and could make those loans quite efficiently because of economies
of scale. At least in Canada, the Grameen approach had become
redundant because the fitness landscape had changed.

When social innovation succeeds, it is no longer innovation, but business as usual. Unlike the product inventor, the fact that that there is no patent for most social innovations, that few may even associate the innovation with them or their organizations, is rarely a source of concern to the people who bring such change about. Rather, it is a source of consolation. For what matters is that the call has been answered, the problem in some way ameliorated.

How to Catch the Moment When Hope and History Rhyme

Nothing is so powerful as an idea whose time has come. But how do we know when our efforts are truly in sync with the times? How does a leader recognize a tipping point? How do we know we are ready to move to the next level? When is it time to leave and start something new—or just leave?

Philanthropic leaders are energized by the possibilities for social transformation, as well they should be. Vision statements are filled with hopes. Then, when hope and history rhyme, social innovation has taken off. But what does the philanthropist do with success? How does he or she move resources into the flow of history? Here's what we suggest:

• Devote resources to identifying and tracking important trends. Make strategic analysis about the connections between local efforts and major trends a regular part of your work.

Funders are in a privileged position to pay attention to trends. People and organizations seeking funding are often immersed in their own local world. Local knowledge and connections are the pillars of grant-seekers' effectiveness, but this local grounding may make them myopic in assessing and understanding larger social, economic and political contexts. Bringing social innovators together to share and compare their observations at the ground level is also a way of identifying trends from the grassroots. Social innovators can then see how what they've identified intersects with what others are detecting at the "grass-tops." Astute funders connect people with these diverse perspectives and require trend analysis in social innovation proposals, literally acting locally but thinking globally.

• Consider supporting social innovators in leaving an initiative once launched successfully; in particular encourage a focus on changing the broader institutional context in order to ensure impact.

There is a time for programs to be dropped as well as started, and for social innovators to move on as well as up. Sustaining a capacity for innovation is different from sustaining a particular innovation or a particular organization. As we saw in the case of PLAN, the best way to create a sea change is often not through replication of the innovation.

—

To policy makers and voluntary-sector organizations, always short on resources, the act of contemplating major trends and big-pictures issues seems both a luxury and an abstraction. But the price is high if they don't—reduced innovation, constrained adaptability and burnout. Nor is the challenge met with larger doses of traditional strategic planning. Such exercises, undertaken periodically at long intervals, are often rote and ritualistic, merely going through the motions of environmental scanning. Static in conception, these sterile encounters are more likely to breed self-congratulation about the road already taken than insight about innovative possibilities in a dynamic and complex world. A practised, ongoing, disciplined and serious process of trend analysis aimed at identifying emerging opportunities and detecting shifts in the landscape can inform both strategic decisions and more immediate tactics.

- Make big-picture, strategic thinking an ongoing part of decision making, not something done only periodically in retreats.

This chapter also offers a cautionary tale for social innovators, those who are out there doing it, creating critical mass and pushing past tipping points. Nothing feels better than knowing you've really gotten past maybe to achieving demonstrable impact. Celebrate, celebrate, celebrate—and then remind yourself to . . .

- Avoid falling prey to and being seduced by success.

Success can create resistance to ongoing change. Both individual practitioners and entire organizations are vulnerable to the rigidities that can follow success. The antidote? Developing a fierce commitment to ongoing reality testing, especially seeking and being open to critical feedback, and standing still to see the bigger picture. This especially behooves those social innovators who think their primary purpose, as visionaries, is always staying upbeat and positive. Instead of cheerleading, cultivate the skills of rigorous pattern analysis and reality testing, which, far from dampening passion, can sharpen vision on the whetstone of mindfulness—paying attention to what is happening and figuring out what it means, becoming ever more adept at distinguishing signal from noise.[21]

- Help social innovators ask not only, Are we doing things right, but also, are we doing the right things?

The focus on increasing effectiveness frequently keeps leaders and evaluators from asking whether the specific program, initiative or strategy is the right thing to be pursuing in the current context. Improving the efficiency and effectiveness of service delivery can divert attention from the question of whether delivering services is the best way to achieve the ultimate goal. Evaluative thinking invites larger strategic questions aimed at assessing the changing fitness landscape.

—

What does this mean for young people interested in making a difference? Throughout this book we've looked at a variety of people who play important roles in bringing about social transformation. All of those roles are open to you: philanthropic leader, policy maker, agency director, social innovator and evaluator. Young people, endless commencement addresses remind us, are the fountain of hope. But they're often short on history. Knowledge of history and the capacity to identify contemporary trends provide a powerful foundation for playing a meaningful role in shaping the future. So to young people we would offer this advice:

• Learn to identify and appreciate the connecting sinew of long past, short past, now, immediate future and distant future. Work these intellectual muscles as if your life depended on it, because it well may, along with the lives of millions of people who could be touched and made better by what you do when you help hope and history rhyme.

Hope and History Redux

In the *Iliad,* Cassandra is described as the loveliest of the daughters of Priam (king of Troy) and gifted with prophecy. The god Apollo loved her, but she spurned him. As a punishment, he decreed that no one from that point on would ever believe her. So when she told her fellow Trojans that the Greeks were hiding inside the wooden horse, they ignored her warning. The irony is that it would have been so easy to check out that possibility, to engage in reality testing. The Cassandra paradox is that the most obvious possibilities may be ignored or dismissed precisely because they are so obvious.

The Trojan Horse was not hard to see. It was huge—right there before their eyes. The large trends affecting us are not always murky, ambiguous and uncertain. Sometimes, perhaps often, they are huge and very visible—but we have to look to see, study closely to distinguish figure from ground, listen carefully to distinguish signal from noise and attune all our senses to detect when hope and history rhyme. Then we need to use all our intellectual powers to interpret the implications of the rhyme. If we do all that, and do it well, we can not only hope for a great sea change, but also help bring such a transformation about.

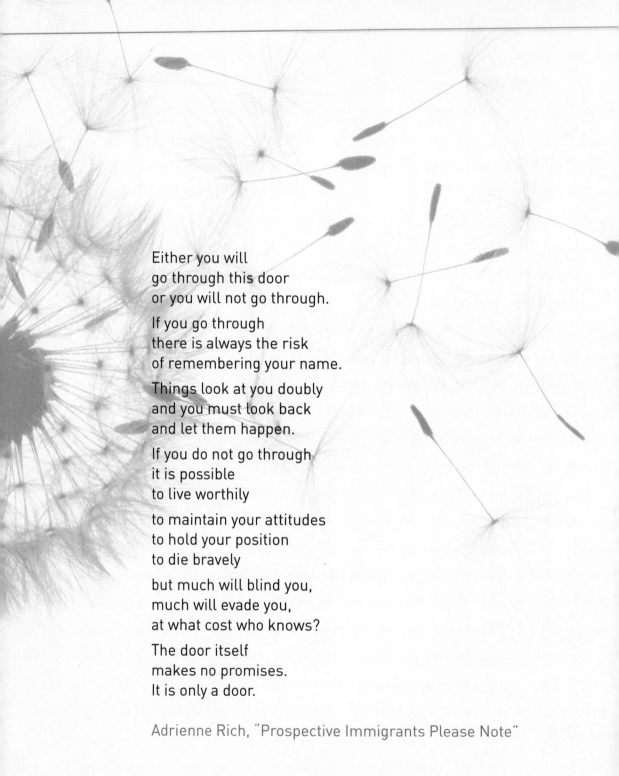

Either you will
go through this door
or you will not go through.

If you go through
there is always the risk
of remembering your name.

Things look at you doubly
and you must look back
and let them happen.

If you do not go through
it is possible
to live worthily

to maintain your attitudes
to hold your position
to die bravely

but much will blind you,
much will evade you,
at what cost who knows?

The door itself
makes no promises.
It is only a door.

Adrienne Rich, "Prospective Immigrants Please Note"

8. The Door Opens

So we come to the end of our journey, or at least the last chapter of this book. The end, from the point of view of social innovation, is often only another beginning, as T.S. Eliot famously said. "And the end of all our exploring / will be to arrive where we started / and know the place for the first time."[1]

We have chosen the poem by Adrienne Rich for this chapter because it contains something of the caution with which we began this book, and something of the hope. It is entitled "Prospective Immigrants Please Note" from her collection *The Fact of the Doorframe,* and for our purposes, it could be called "Prospective Innovators Please Note." Innovators, like immigrants, often take great risks. Going to a new place inevitably means leaving something behind. Moreover, there is no guarantee of success. Still, innovators, like immigrants, feel compelled to take the step because they can no longer tolerate the place where they are. They see the door, the opening, and they step through.

As the poem says, the door makes no promises; it is only a door. There exists, all around us, the possibility of stepping across a threshold—from helplessness to action, from caution to belief, from ignorance to knowledge. The social innovators we have described in this book have all stepped across such thresholds and they tell us that *doors are constantly opening. If you miss one you'll find another. That's the good news.*

The less good news, at least for some, is that there is no formula for knowing which door is the right door; indeed, the notion of "maybe" is that there is no right door. It is just a door. There is no road map for social innovation; it is not a route that can be mapped step by step.

Have you ever been in an old house that seems to have grown rather than being built? The house begins as a single room with windows and a door. As the years pass and prosperity increases, a second, much more gracious room is added. This then seems a much more prepossessing way to enter the house, so an outside door is added to this room, too. But when a kitchen is added in the back, the "real" door is built there, where friends and family enter. Later, a second wing is added and yet another door. Each room has a door; each room is different—a unique space; all the rooms in the house are interconnected.

Social innovation is much like that house, with recognizable rooms, each with its own character and connected by a number of doors. Whatever room you find yourself in, you know that the other rooms exist and that you are likely to pass through them, sometimes repeatedly. Most of you will recognize at least one of the metaphoric rooms we have described in this book. You will have aspired to *maybe*, or *stood still*, or engaged the *powerful stranger*, or been found by *flow*, or hit bottom in *cold heaven*, or felt the moment when *hope and history rhyme*. Whether you are someone standing at the threshold of your first initiative, or at midstream

in a project, or frustrated after a life of efforts to change things, we wrote
this book to give you a sense that these experiences are connected.

The social innovators we describe all walked through doors when they
began their initiatives. But there were also doors they didn't go through,
and some that led to places they didn't want to be. Al Etmanski from
PLAN sums up this experience:

> I think if the goal is getting to maybe, then the doors open
> often. Doors open all of the time. My sense is that in our
> lives we've missed all kinds of doors because we haven't been
> standing still. So there's the paradox there, because on the
> other hand, they may not have been the right doors, they may
> not have been the doors we thought they were. What we
> missed may not have been important or what we missed may
> have been very important.

Social innovators are not people who create more doors, or even people
who are surrounded by more doors than other folks. They are simply
people who *see* more doors. They *believe* in doors, if you will, and so
doors are there. The difference between Lucy and Edmund in
C.S. Lewis's *The Lion, the Witch and the Wardrobe* was that at first Lucy
believed in the possibility of the wardrobe and Edmund did not. Over
time, of course, social innovators become more practised at the art of
seeing doors, and even at knowing which ones offer the promise of
getting to maybe. But how do they deal with the kind of uncertainty that
Etmanski describes? Over time they seem to get more comfortable with
the choosing and the not choosing. They prepare; they are poised; they
respond. For Deanna Foster, from the Hope Community, this is what
being a strategic explorer is all about. "One of the dangers is to get
compromised and drawn off course by new things that come along

that don't build on our strategy," she says. "Things that emerge have been thought about and nurtured for a long time. Either the work is building toward an opening for a new opportunity, or we have talked and strategized about something over and over again. When that's the case, we're right there. If the opportunity's there, we're on it and it's done. People think that's impulsive, and it's totally the opposite—it is strategic."

We have many proverbs and maxims to express this relationship between preparedness and opportunity, skill and luck. *Chance favours the mind prepared. God helps those who help themselves. When opportunity knocks open the door. There is a tide in the affairs of men when taken at the flood leads on to fortune.* Our complexity framework gives form and substance to what has long been folk wisdom. Over time, with practice, the choice becomes easier. But how do we begin? In that house with many doors, in a world where opportunities for action are all around us, how do we know which door to walk through, and when?

Part of the answer may lie in what happens to us when we don't walk through. "If you do not go through. . ." Adrienne Rich writes, "much will blind you, / much will evade you." In particular, you may not remember your name, who you are, why you are here. The thing about hearing a call is that it fetches *you* forth: your deepest convictions, capacities and emotions. The world calls and if you don't respond, you risk leaving your potential unrealized. And, conversely, if you don't know who you are (and we all lose track of that sometimes), then you should probably start looking for doors to step through.

Begin where you are—this is what the stories of Bob Gelfdof and Linda Lundström tell us so clearly. Sometimes any action, small or large, is better than none. There comes a time to tie the rock to your ankle and throw it over the cliff. Just do it. Even if you aren't sure exactly what is at the bottom.

Perhaps the most important thing about social innovation is that, like exploration or immigration, it demands simultaneously that we set a course, move to action and relinquish the idea that we can control the outcome. Deanna Foster brings as much knowledge to bear on a situation as she can and then acts; Al Etmanski tells us that action sometimes precedes knowledge. Getting comfortable with acting in the face of uncertainty is part of being an explorer.

After reading explorer Francis Chichester's autobiography, Peter Vaill, who made a life of helping organizations look into the future, created a fictional dialogue to illustrate the nature of exploration. Chichester is being interviewed by an MBA student anxious to learn how to become an explorer:

C: Let me try to say this in a way that will convey my feeling as an explorer. I did not have the port [in mind] the way you insist that I had it along the way. What I had was a going-forward-toward. That going-forward-toward was a good deal more general than you imagine. It is the non-explorers who rather naively assume that once they have a clear sharp picture in mind of where they are going, they can trust that picture through to the end. To be an explorer is to not know where, precisely and concretely, one is going.
MBA: Going-forward-toward. Beats me.
C: When you go through your dark living room on the way to the kitchen at 3 a.m., do you simply stride confidently across the floor?

MBA: Not unless I want to fall over the dog or crunch a toe on the coffee table.

C: What is your mind doing as you cross the room?

MBA: Feeling for the dog and the corner of the table.

C: Somewhat tentatively?

MBA: Yes.

C: Where is the kitchen, in your mind?

MBA: In my mind, it's . . . it's there but it's . . .

C: Somewhat subordinate to the more immediate concerns of the dog and the coffee table?

MBA: Yes, I guess so.

C: If you smelled a strong feces smell as you entered the darkened room, what would you do?

MBA: I would turn on the light.

C: For the obvious reason.

MBA: For the obvious reason.

C: The dog and the coffee table in turn become subordinate to yet a more immediate concern?

MBA: Yes. But I'm still trying to get to the kitchen.

C: Yes, you are still trying to get to the kitchen. You are going-forward-toward it. That is precisely the way a "port" is for me, right up to the point that I actually alight on the wharf. Meanwhile, along the way, as you say, a host of more immediate concerns occupy me, concerns with which I deal as best I can, sometimes neatly, but more often with the most precarious feeling of makeshift. That is what it is to be an explorer.[2]

Obstacles and uncertainties. Multiple choices; multiple doors. They abound in social innovation. And ultimately, they mean that like Chichester's explorations, social innovation is much more about going-forward-toward than it is about arriving at a specific destination, imagined in advance. Looking back on their own journeys, their own initiatives, the social innovators, like Chichester, do not radiate any particular feeling of "mission accomplished." Rather, when looking back (and it should be mentioned that looking back doesn't seem to be their favourite occupation), they are sure about change but unsure about their own role.

Years after Balfour Mount introduced his vision of palliative care to the Royal Victoria, after he had left the service in the hands of others, he observed that while the number of palliative care beds across Canada continued to rise, some elements of the original vision seemed to have been lost. Remember that for those who began the palliative care movement, it wasn't only about preventing pain in terminally ill patients. It was also about treating mind, body and *spirit*. Medical culture in large teaching hospitals is a powerful thing, however, and proved a limiting

factor to this particular vision of the care of people at the end of life. "The risk on the part of the medical profession, even those involved in palliative care, is of becoming simply 'symptomatologists,'" Mount notes, "hence missing the significance of the existential/spiritual concerns that shape our response to all life experiences." However, despite the loss of this radical edge in palliative care, Mount is in no way discouraged. He focuses instead on the signs of a marked change in medicine as a whole. "Recent research," he notes, "has continued to demonstrate the interdependence of body, mind and spirit, and there is increasing interest in the notion of 'healing' in mainstream medicine. Healing is understood here as a quality of life shift toward a sense of integrity and wholeness and away from anguish and suffering. You can die healed! Indeed, McGill medical school is now redesigning its medical curriculum to include emphasis on healing throughout the four-year program." Because the place you arrive is not what you expected when you started out does not mean your journey has failed. System transformations often surprise the very people who set out to create them.

For Rusty Pritchard, things are now possible in the Atlanta community into which he and Joanna moved that were never possible before. He told us:

> Months after the last crack house on the street closed down, some gang members returned from prison and tried to retake the street. They marched up the street and unloaded a shotgun at a group of high-schoolers who had disrespected them the previous day (by telling them not to drive up and down the street so fast!), hitting one and causing him to nearly lose his leg. The neighbourhood rallied in a way that amazed everyone, including the older residents, to signal that this was no longer that kind of neighbourhood. The two first on the scene to give Demetrius first aid were me and the white policewoman who lived next door; I applied pressure to the wounds while she gave mouth-to-mouth CPR—the sort of thing people expected from rescue personnel but not from neighbors. Everyone knew it was care and not just a job. The outside prayer vigil the next day was a picture of what we think heaven will be like—all races, ages, classes, joining together in common purpose.

This story would seem like success . . . distinct, clear, tangible. And yet, is this exactly what Rusty and Joanna expected when they stepped through the door into the community that was to be their new home? Do they feel confident that their own actions produced this kind of sea change? They are clear that this could have not happened without flow; and that means they themselves were part of a pattern, not its generator.

Social innovation is often a discovery, even to those involved. When you arrive at that new place, and know it for the first time, and it is different from the destination you had in mind, is it still a success? Is it a success to which you contributed? Surely, these social innovators must have deep pride in their accomplishments. But listen to Paul Born, reflecting on his experience with OP2000:

> A story appeared on the front page of the Saturday edition of the *Kitchener-Waterloo Record* on Easter weekend, about a study done by Statistics Canada which showed that in 1980, the region had 6 per cent more poor people than an average metropolitan area. By 2000, the region had 12 percent fewer poor people than an average urban area.
>
> Was Opportunities 2000 responsible for the incredible news found in the paper on this Easter weekend? Not solely.
>
> The question we ask ourselves is what role did Opportunities 2000 play in this incredible community achievement of reducing our poverty rate to the lowest in Canada? As the article does not even mention the campaign, it would be easy to say, "Very little." And of course in the overall scope of the dynamic economy and winning attitude of this place called Waterloo region the impact of a four-year campaign is minimal. Or is it?
>
> In a sense it is the chicken or the egg question. Was Opportunities 2000 responsible for reducing poverty to the lowest level in Canada or was the spirit and attitude of Waterloo region responsible for founding Opportunities 2000? I would suggest it was the latter. In a community where people deeply care and embrace bold ideas, the rally to reduce poverty, as a community-wide millennium goal, is not surprising. We already had the second-lowest poverty rate in

the country when the goal was declared and our clear desire
to be the best was the essence of the call. It was the
motivating force.

If you are getting ready to step through the doorway, to try your hand at
changing even a small part of the world, the lack of certainty expressed
by Pritchard, Mount and Born may give you pause. Is it worth it to set
out on this journey that might have no end (or at least not the one you
imagined)? Especially since even if you are successful in completing
the journey, you might never be able to tell if your efforts made a
difference?

We can only repeat that getting to maybe isn't about certainty. And, as
our social innovators tell us, attributing praise or blame in a complex
process merely confuses things. For here is the last paradox of social
innovation: although we have spent a whole book telling you that it is
all about you—your sense of calling, your fears and your dreams—it
also *isn't about you*. Ulysses Seal knew this paradox well. He would laugh
when concerned members talked about cloning him so that
the organization would remain vital. He always felt that whether the
organization survived him or not, the people and the ideas that were the
basis for innovation would continue to create the kind of change needed
for conservation. It wasn't about him.

Just weeks before his death in 2003, an interviewer asked Seal whether
he had any regrets. Remember, this is the man who spent his life first
searching for treatments for human cancers and then trying to save
endangered species. Seal didn't say that he wondered, since the cure for
cancer and the cure for species extinction both remain elusive, if his was
a life well spent. In fact, at first it seemed as if he wouldn't answer the
question at all. He talked instead of his belief that something important,

a sea change actually, was about to happen. "There is a lot of work left to be done," he admitted, "both with respect to the species and to people's commitment. My sense is, though, that there is a major expanding commitment to conservation. We are at a hinge point—there is a cusp occurring here now—and there are things we can do to help change the ultimate outcomes." Then at last he returned to the question. "If there is a regret, it's that I'm not going to be able to participate in that change further down the road," Seal mused. "I don't really spend much time on regrets except in the sense that I'm going to miss all the fun."[3]

There are no perfect people. There are no perfect projects. We are not measured against perfection, only called to do what we can, to set out on an exploration to an imagined destination, an imagined good. So forget about the fear, forget about the guilt, forget about the fact that the doorway makes no promises. Just step through. Don't miss all the fun.

As Yeats wrote, near the end of his life:

> when such as I cast out remorse
> so great a sweetness flows into the breast
> we must laugh and we must sing
> we are blest by everything
> everything we look upon is blest."[4]

Getting to maybe doesn't get any better than that.

Notes

I. THE FIRST LIGHT OF EVENING

1. The case of Live Aid is drawn from Bob Geldof's autobiography, *Is That It?* (London: Penguin, 1986), and from various newspaper accounts of the event. See also F. Westley, "Bob Geldof and Live Aid: The Affective Side of Global Social Innovation," *Human Relations* 44, 10 (1991): 1011–1036.

2. World Bank, *Controlling AIDS: Public Priorities in a Global Epidemic* (New York: Oxford University Press, 1997).

3. For additional information on the background of the Brazil case please refer to James Begun, Brenda Zimmerman and Kevin Dooley, "Health Care Organizations as Complex Adaptive Systems," S.M. Mick and M. Wyttenbach (eds), *Advances in Health Care Organization Theory* (San Francisco: Jossey-Bass, 2003): 253–288.

4. Adapted from S. Glouberman and B. Zimmerman, "Complicated and Complex Systems: What Would Successful Reform of Medicine Look Like," in P.G. Forest, T. Mckintosh and G. Marchilden (eds), *Health Care Services and the Process of Change* (Toronto: University of Toronto Press, 2004): 5.

5. Ibid., 26–53.

6. Ibid., 5.

7. This idea from E. Young, unpublished speech, "Policy Learning and Distributed Governance: Lessons from Canada and the U.K.," June 5, 2003, Canadian High Commission/Demos Conference, London, UK.

8. For more information on Linda Lundström, please see www.lindalundstrom.com.

9. The case of Rusty Pritchard is drawn from personal interviews.

10. John Perkins, *Let Justice Roll Down* (Regal Books,1976), and Robert Lupton, *Theirs Is the Kingdom* (New York: Harper and Row, 1989). See also www.ccda.org.

11. Jonathan Crane, "The Epidemic Theory of Ghettos and Neighborhood Effects on Dropping Out," *American Journal of Sociology* 95,5 (1989):1226–1254.

12. Hannah Arendt, *Between Past and Future: Eight Exercises in Political Thought* (New York: Viking, 1968), 4.

13. R. Fisher and W. Ury, *Getting to Yes: Negotiating Agreement without Giving In* (New York: Penguin, 1983).

2. GETTING TO MAYBE

1. The case of Reverend Jeffrey Brown was composed in part by Nada Farah, based on a presentation by Jeff Brown at McGill University in March 2003, and in part is drawn from Alexis Gendron and Kathleen Valley, 2000, Harvard Business School Case, "Reverend Jeffrey Brown: Cops, Kids and Ministers."

2. Jenny Berrien describes how the police chose to ignore the issue of youth violence in order to avoid acknowledging that Boston, like New York, Chicago and other major U.S. cities, was becoming a pool of drug and gang crime. "The Boston Miracle: The Emergence of New Institutional Structures in the Absence of Rational Planning," honours thesis, Harvard College, March 1997.

3. Alexis Gendron and Kathleen Valley highlighted in "Reverend Jeffrey Brown" that the mistrust between the black community and the white Irish police, or Irish Mob as the police was called then, was also due to the lack of common ground between the two groups.

4. Brown described the details of the Morning Star incident. Dan Kennedy, in his article "The Best: Local Heroes" for the *Boston Phoenix*, June 11, 1996, detailed the incident and provided us with the name of the victim as well as the exact date the attack occurred.

5. For more information on the TenPoint Coalition, see www.bostontenpoint.org.

6. Geldof, *Is That It?* 271.

7. Robert Frost, "Two Tramps in Mud Time," in *The Complete Poems of Robert Frost* (New York: Holt Rine and Winston, 1967), 359.

8. The story of Edward Lorenz's discovery is told in many books, including James Gleick, *Chaos: Making of a New Science* (New York: Viking), 1987.

9. Jonathan Patz et al., "Impact of Regional Climate Change on Human Health," *Nature*, November 17, 2005, 1–8.

3. STAND STILL

1. We have drawn from two primary books for the story of the Grameen Bank and Muhammad Yunus: David Bornstein, *The Price of a Dream: The Story of the Grameen Bank* (Oxford: Oxford University Press, 1996), and Muhammad Yunus, *Banker to the Poor: Micro-Lending and the Battle against World Poverty* (New York: Public Affairs, 1999). Further information on the Grameen Bank can be found at www.grameen-info.org/bank.

2. Yunus, *Banker to the Poor*, 34.

3. Ibid., 48.

4. Ibid., 63.

5. David Bornstein, *How to Change the World* (New York: Oxford University Press, 2004).

6. Yunus, *Banker to the Poor*, 35–36.

7. Parker Palmer, *The Active Life* (San Francisco: Jossey-Bass, 1990), 55–56.

8. Ibid., 55–56.

9. The idea of resilience is drawn from the work of C.S. Holling and his colleagues at the Resilience Alliance. In 2002, they brought together many scholars to address the panarchy model in L.H. Gunderson and C.S. Holling (eds), *Panarchy: Understanding Transformations in Human and Natural Systems* (Washington, D.C.: Island Press).

10. Adapted from diagram on the Resilience Alliance website. See http://www.resalliance.org/570.php.

11. Danny Miller, *The Icarus Paradox: How Exceptional Companies Bring about Their Own Demise* (New York: HarperCollins, 1992).

12. The story of PLAN is paraphrased and cited from the case, "Voice and Ground: Social Innovation at the Planned Lifetime Advocacy Network (PLAN)," prepared and written for this project by Warren Nilsson, research assistant to the think-tank, under the direction of Frances Westley. Warren Nilsson is a doctoral candidate at McGill University's Desautels Faculty of Management. Further information on PLAN is available at www.plan.ca.

13. T. Kuntz, "What Keeps Us Safe: The Care between Citizens" *Abilities* (Winter 2001): 40–41.

4. THE POWERFUL STRANGERS

1. W.B. Yeats, "Remorse for Intemperate Speech," quoted in Geldof, *Is That It?*

2. Complexity theorists describe such distribution as "power law"—the lumpy, uneven distribution of connections that characterize self-organizing systems on the edge of chaos. The most cited case of this kind of "power law" distribution is the Internet. Sites on the Internet that are visited most often move up the hierarchy in

search engines and so are visited yet more often. A pattern emerges of star sites, visited much more often than average, and a clear divide arises (as opposed to a continuous hierarchy) between the "haves" and the "have-nots." Hence the notion of a power law: the pattern is not one of smooth increases, but of discontinuities of great magnitude, in mathematical language "raised to the power of *x*."

Simple comparisons of two types of distribution are shown in figures 1 and 2 below. In figure 1, we see a bell distribution, which is called a "normal" distribution. In this case, the average also represents a highly likely state. Most cases cluster around the average. The further one is away from the average, the fewer cases there are. This is the case for either tail, for either side of the average. Figure 1 could represent how many houses are on a block in a neighbourhood. Here we see a few blocks with very few homes, four or five. There are about the same number with many more than the average, fifteen or sixteen. But most cluster around the average and the tails disappear quite quickly. Most blocks have ten houses, give or take a house or two. The average becomes a very significant descriptor. To say the average block in this community has ten houses gives a pretty good description of the housing density in the neighbourhood. We see the same type of distribution in heights of people. The average height is a useful means to describe a population. Most cluster around the average and one would not imagine, other than in horror movies or fantasy books, a person who is ten times the average height or ten times smaller than the average. But in Figure 2, we see a power law distribution where there is no clustering around an average. To say the average website has *x* number of incoming links is quite meaningless when most sites have only one or fewer links and a small number of sites have ten thousand incoming links. Distribution of connectedness on the web is very lumpy, indeed.

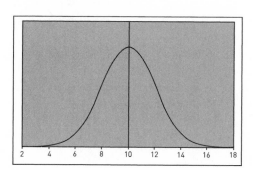

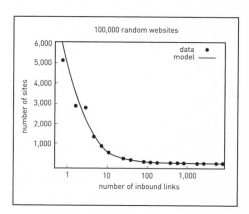

Figure 1: A normal distribution or bell curve   Figure 2: Power law distribution of websites

Power law patterns are created not through the action of any individual but as a result of multiple micro-level choices. Some systems characterized by power laws, such as the uneven utilization of words (with some words used much more often than others), are subject to "tipping points," sudden reconfigurations based on fads, epidemics, etc. We will consider this phenomenon further in the next chapter. In this chapter, it is important to recognize that other systems characterized by power laws are probably more resistant to tipping points. It would appear that once the distribution of the resources for creating and maintaining a particular social order take on a power law or "haves and have-nots" quality, that social system is resistant to change. "The rich get richer and the poor get poorer" is the maxim commonly used to capture this characteristic. The hubs, once formed, seek to maintain themselves.

3. Leonard Cohen and Sharon Robinson, "Everybody Knows," from the album *Cohen Live*. Stranger Music Inc. (BMI), 1988.

4. The HIV/AIDS case was drawn from a detailed study of the dynamics of interaction of the different groups involved in changing the approach to HIV/AIDS treatment. For a fuller discussion see S. Maguire, N. Phillips, and C. Hardy, "When 'Silence = Death,' Keep Talking: Trust, Control and the Discursive Construction of Identity in the Canadian HIV/AIDS Treatment Domain," *Organization Studies*, 22,2 (2001): 287–312.

5. Ibid., 300.

6. Ibid.

7. Ibid., 309.

8. F. Westley, " Not on our Watch: The Biodiversity Crisis and Global Collaborative Response," in D.L Cooperrider and J.E. Dutton (eds), *Organizational Dimensions of Global Change* (Thousand Oaks, Sage Publications, 1999), 88–113.

9. The case of Ulysses Seal and CBSG is drawn from personal interviews and from earlier writings including F. Westley and H. Vredenburg, "Interorganizational Collaboration and the Preservation of Global Biodiversity," *Organization Science* 8, 4 (1997), 381–403. For more information on CBSG and its activities see www.cbsg.org.

10. K. Alvarez, *The Twilight of the Panther* (Sarasota, FL: Myakka River, 1994.), 447.

11. The case of Mary Gordon and Roots of Empathy was drawn from personal interviews and Amy Eldon's interview with Mary Gordon for the PBS series *Global Tribe*, at www.pds.org/kcet/globaltribe. For further information on Roots of Empathy, see www.rootsofempathy.org.

12. Russell Daye, *Political Forgiveness: Lessons from South Africa* (New York: Orbis Books, 2004).

13. We have drawn from various works of Cicely Saunders including "The Evolution of Palliative Care," *Patient Education and Counseling* 41 (2000): 7; "A Personal Therapeutic Journey," *British Medical Journal* 313, no. 7072 (1996),

http://bmj.bmjjournals.com; and Cicely Saunders, Dorothy H. Summers and Neville Teller (eds), *Hospice: The Living Idea* (London: Edward Arnold, 1981).

14. Robert G. Twycross, "Palliative Care: An International Necessity," *Journal of Pain and Palliative Care Pharmacotherapy* 16, 1 (2002), 5-79.

15. The case of Dr. Balfour Mount is drawn from an article by Frances Westley, "Vision Worlds," *Advances in Strategic Management*, 8 (1992): 271–306.

5. LET IT FIND YOU

1. Geldof, *Is That It?* 281.

2. M. Czikszentmihaly, *Finding Flow* (New York: Basic Books, 1997).

3. Ibid., 30–31.

4. Interview with Edwin Land. For fuller account, see F. Westley and H. Mintzberg, "Visionary Leadership and Strategic Management," *Strategic Management Journal* 19, 2 (1989): 134–143.

5. E. Durkheim, *The Elementary Forms of the Religious Life* (New York: Free Press, 1965), 134.

6. Steven Johnson, *Emergence: The Connected Lives of Ants, Brains, Cities and Software* (New York: Scribner, 2001).

7. These examples of *dagu* were provided by C.Y. Gopinath from PATH in Nairobi. Used with his permission.

8. A. Downie, "Brazil: Showing Others the Way," *San Francisco Chronicle*, March 25, 2001, www.aegis.org/news/sc/2001/sc010310.html.

9. Paulo Freire, *Pedagogy of the Oppressed* (New York: Continuum, 1970).

10. Glouberman, and Zimmerman, "Complicated and Complex Systems."

11. Jane Jacobs is the author of many books including *The Death and Life of Great American Cities* (New York: Vintage Books, 1951); *Dark Age Ahead,* (New York: Vintage Books, 2005) ; and *Systems of Survival* (New York: Vintage Books, 1994).

12. Malcolm Gladwell, *The Tipping Point* (New York: Little Brown and Co., 2000).

13. Henry Mintzberg, "Crafting Strategy," *Harvard Business Review* 65, 4 (1987): 66–76.

14. E. Helpman and Paul Krugman, *Market Structure and Foreign Trade* (Cambridge, MA: MIT Press, 1985.)

15. The case of Paul Born and OP2000 is drawn from personal interviews and from D. McNair and E. Leviten-Reid, "A Radical Notion," *Making Waves* 13, 3 (2002): 19–29. For Paul Born's current initiatives, go to www.tamarackcommunity.ca.

16. For a fuller discussion of improvisation see Karl Weick, "Improvisation as a Mindset for Organizational Analysis," *Organization Science* 9 (September/October 1998): 543–555. The simplistic understanding of improvisation ("making something out of nothing") belies the discipline and experience on which improvisers depend, and it obscures the actual practices and processes that engage them. Improvisation depends,

in fact, on thinkers having absorbed a broad base of knowledge, including myriad conventions that contribute to formulating ideas logically, cogently and expressively.
17. Weick coined the term "heedfulness" to address intense listening that happens in groups when they are being mindful of the emerging patterns at multiple levels.
18. P. Berliner, *Thinking in Jazz: The Infinite Art of Improvization* (Chicago: University of Chicago Press, 1994), 401.
19. One source of information for sharing comes from evaluation. Standard practice in evaluation, as in research generally, is to carefully develop all data collection protocols and procedures prior to fieldwork. This is sensible in that it ensures that the appropriate and relevant data will be collected in a way that is valid and reliable. Sampling, instrumentation, interview and survey questions, statistical indicators analysis procedures are all specified in the design. The problem is that this assumes one can predetermine what is appropriate, relevant and useful. Evaluating emergent phenomena, like social innovation, requires emergent evaluation designs. This means snowball sampling (building the sample along the way as information accumulates and new sources of data are discovered), adapting inquiry questions and instrumentation as initial results come in, and using rapid appraisal techniques, quick analysis, ongoing feedback and open-ended fieldwork in search of the unanticipated. These are not standard evaluation operating procedures but they are essential if the evaluator is to be open to letting crucial information emerge and, in a very real sense, find the evaluator. Evaluation information can both reveal flow and be part of flow, the latter when the data seem to come pouring in and the evaluator is racing to keep up with what's emerging. Instead of the usual drudgery and meaningless paperwork associated with most evaluations, real *in the flow* evaluative data collection and feedback contributes to the excitement of learning and the anticipation and realization of new understandings that inform the next steps in the innovation process.

6. COLD HEAVEN

1. See Terry J. Allen, "The General and the Genocide: General Roméo Dallaire," *Amnesty International NOW Magazine*, Winter 2002, available at www.thirdworldtraveler.com; Roméo A. Dallaire and Brent Beardsley, *Shake Hands with the Devil: The Failure of Humanity in Rwanda* (Toronto: Random House Canada, 2004).
2. Tana Dineen, "The Solitary, Tortured Nobility of Roméo Dallaire," *Ottawa Citizen*, July 13, 2000. Retrieved May 2, 2006, from http://tanadineen.com.
3. Roméo Dallaire, "Speaking Truth to Power," keynote address and follow-up fireside chat at "Crossing Borders, Crossing Boundaries," Joint International Evaluation Conference of the Canadian Evaluation Society and the American Evaluation Association, Toronto, November 5, 2005. See also Dallaire and Beardsley,

Shake Hands with the Devil.

4. Born's innovative community engagement institute: http://tamarackcommunity.ca.

5. From personal interview with Paul Born.

6. Westley, "Not on Our Watch," 102.

7. Jim Collins, *Good to Great: Why Some Companies Make the Leap . . . and Others Don't* (New York: HarperBusiness, 2001).

8. Such step-by-step specification from inputs through activities to outputs and outcomes is called a logic model. Logic models have become a common requirement for funding proposals submitted to major philanthropic foundations. In some cases this specification is called a theory of change or program theory. All such conceptualizations require the pretense of prior knowledge about exactly how an innovation will unfold. In highly emergent, complex environments such prior specification is neither possible nor desirable because it constrains openness and adaptability. Developmental evaluation is an alternative that embraces emergence and complexity.

9. Dorothy Day founded the Catholic Worker movement. For more information on her life see Jim Forest, "A Biography of Dorothy Day," on Paulist Father's website, www.paulist.org/dorothyday/ddaybio.html.

10. Interview on Minnesota Public Radio, November 17, 2004: http://news.minnesota.publicradio.org/features/2004/11/17_olsond_development/.

11. Deanne Foster and Mary Keefe, "Hope Community: The Power of People and Place," in McKnight Foundation, *End of One Way* (Minneapolis, MN: McKnight Foundation, 2004), 34.

12. Interview by Michael Patton.

13. Ibid.

14. Ibid.

15. Foster and Keefer, "Hope Community: The Power of People and Place."

16. Evaluators tend to give highest prestige to "summative" evaluations, those focused on judging the overall merit, worth and significance of a program, and determining whether the program worked as specified in its logic model, including whether the targeted goals were attained. In contrast, "formative" evaluations are conducted to improve a program, identify strengths and weaknesses, and ready the program for the rigorous demands of summative evaluation. Hope's questions differ from the usual type of formative evaluations because Hope's leadership focused on an open-ended approach to data gathering, where the questions and concerns were emergent, and where trial and error was carefully mined for learning against a backdrop of changing goals as what the leadership understood was needed and possible changed within the context of their larger vision and values.

17. Foster and Keefe, "Hope Community: The Power of People and Place," 40.

18. For more on the organization and its history see www.damianocenter.org.

19. See www.amizade.org/Countries/DC.htm.

20. A more in-depth discussion of developmental evaluation in relation to complexity science may be helpful to those involved in implementing such an approach. The non-linear nature of emergent social innovation gives rise to inherent tensions in the struggle to figure out what it means to be successful. These tensions can be considered as paradoxes. Paradox was a regularly recurring theme in the stories of social innovation we heard. We found particularly challenging paradoxes appearing in the encounter with cold heaven, that is, in attempting to identify, understand and learn from what is and is not working, and the consequences of interpreting something as success or failure.

Chapter 3, "Stand Still," highlighted the marriage of inquiry and action, that is, action as a form of inquiry and inquiry as a form of action. Traditional evaluation insists on separating evaluative inquiry from action by making the evaluation external to the intervention and making the evaluator independent of and distant from those engaged in bringing about change. Complexity-based, developmental evaluation joins inquiry and action in the challenge of being simultaneously engaged and reflective, open and evaluative, and fiercely committed by being fiercely skeptical.

Another evaluative tension surfaces in being simultaneously goal oriented and open to emergence. Inherent in the notion that something has succeeded or failed is the idea that something desired (usually called a goal or intended outcome) was or was not attained. But in complex, non-linear, emergent processes, direction can be fluid, ambiguous and ever evolving. Paradoxically, openness to what emerges *becomes* the goal, even though one is simultaneously moving forward toward an envisioned future. Acknowledging and embracing this tension opens the social innovator to evaluating short-term desired outcomes (how and where are we making progress?) while also rigorously watching out for unanticipated consequences, unpredicted (and unpredictable) side effects, spinoffs and ripples emanating from interventions (what is happening around and beyond our hoped-for results?). The narrow goal orientation of much traditional evaluation can result in missing such important unanticipated outcomes. To be sure, a major effort at social innovation is likely to have both short-term objectives along the way (here's what we hope to accomplish in the next six months) and a long-term vision, but along the journey complexity theory alerts us to be mindful of the unexpected, and emergent. Moreover, the language used in traditional evaluation, which talks of "side effects" or "secondary effects," "unexpected results" and "unanticipated consequences," tends to be dismissive of outcomes that might, in fact, be crucial achievements or reveal opportunities for critical learning. While traditional evaluation judges mistakes and unattained objectives as failures, developmental evaluation treats them as learning opportunities and chances to make corrections or to take a new path.

As Chapter 4, "The Powerful Strangers," highlighted, power relationships are transformed when social innovation processes are based on complexity insights. There are tensions here between maintaining and giving up control, between knowing where you are going and being open to where the process takes you, and between being part of the unfolding process even as you stand outside of and evaluate that unfolding process. Ongoing, intensifying interactions and deepening relationships replace formal and traditional forms of control (such as the determined implementation of an ordained plan or adherence to an approved evaluation design with specified samples and measures). Monitoring through interaction and relationship involves both a different kind of control (because it becomes relational and interdependent) and relinquishing control for the same reason. Evaluators have traditionally been admonished to remain external, independent and objective, but complexity-based developmental evaluation recognizes that data collection is a form of action and intervention, that the act of observation changes what is observed and that the observer can never really remain outside of and external to what he observes. The evaluator gives up the control that typically resides in rigid, preordained designs in order to experience and gain insight from observations (both anticipated in the design and emergent beyond the formal design) that come only from standing closer to and in relationship with the action and the primary actors. Moreover, even the roles shift, for the actors and innovators are simultaneously (and paradoxically) both the evaluated and the evaluators, and the developmental evaluation facilitator, by entering actively into the arena, even as an observer, becomes part of the action and therefore part of the intervention.

Tension resides in the paradox of, on the one hand, accepting constrained personal power and responsibility in the face of larger system dynamics and macro forces and yet, on the other hand, believing that individuals can make a difference and are responsible and acting accordingly. Evaluation, then, in a complexity framework, should encourage cross-scale and micro-macro reflections in order to facilitate learning about the effectiveness of discrete micro actions and the implications of those actions in relation to larger uncontrollable macro forces and trends. Developmental evaluators work with social innovators to look closely at and understand apparent "failure" at the personal level at different levels of analysis including in the context of larger macro forces, and provide an opportunity for "standing still" and learning, hopefully an antidote to cold heaven despair, and perhaps even a bridge to renewed commitment and action.

The tension in evaluation between learning and accountability is often palpable. Accountability is traditionally focused on compliance with prescribed and approved procedures and attaining intended results. Learning, in this framework, becomes learning about how best to attain the desired outcomes—and only that. This leaves little or no space to learn that the intended outcomes were inappropriate or less important than new, emergent possibilities. Failure as defined in traditional evaluation (as goals not attained) becomes reframed as feedback from a complexity perspective. This is captured in the complexity conclusion: it didn't work—which means it worked. What didn't work was our fallible effort at change. What did work was the "system"; the world unfolded as it is wont to unfold. Knowing that allows us to approach and reframe seeming failure as an opportunity to learn, regroup and take another shot. *The only real failure is the failure to learn.* Accountability shifts from compliance to learning: not just any learning, but learning that bears the burden of demonstrating that it can, does and will inform future action.

We would add here that performance indicators, though all the rage in government, offer little in the way of real accountability. Crime rates, unemployment rates and standardized achievement tests in education offer important insights about trends, but those data require interpretation. That's where things get tricky. In both the private and public sectors, we have seen the manipulation and corruption of indicators where the stakes are high: think of Enron manipulating its quarterly profit reports or the manipulation and distortion of supposedly objective "intelligence analysis" used to justify the invasion of Iraq. Preoccupation with measuring a few indicators creates a kind of tunnel vision that shuts out the complexity of reality. Things appear simpler and more controllable than they are. Interpreting indicators in a broader context means not just knowing whether the number has changed but delving into why it has changed, what the change means and what other changes are occurring at the sample time. That moves the interpretation from simple to complex.

Interpretations of performance indicators are greatly enhanced by incorporating other evaluation methods. Using mixed methods, multiple sources and diverse lenses to engage in deep reality testing will usually yield a complex picture of change. Quantitative data on trends and outcomes need to be contextualized and interpreted in the light of qualitative observations and purposefully sampled case studies. All data sources and informants come with errors and limitations, so multiple sources must be filtered and aggregated to build more holistic understandings of dynamic systems. Diverse interpretive lenses and theoretical frameworks guard against the disease of "the hardening of the categories," where one forces all data through a narrow, predetermined way of making sense of complex systems.

21. Professional evaluators have an important role to play in supporting reflective practice and ongoing learning, and maintaining a sense of perspective—if they are willing and able to engage in developmental evaluation. But evaluators often hinder social innovation by imposing overly rigid designs and aiming at definitive judgments to satisfy narrow accountability demands. It is important to be sure that the nature of the evaluation matches the nature of the social innovation. We caution evaluators not to impose summative evaluation designs on developmental innovations. More broadly, evaluators and those who fund evaluation need to remain clear about different evaluation purposes and the importance of matching evaluation processes and designs to the nature of the intervention.

Where learning has a high priority, the evaluator can play a role in facilitating learning and helping those involved avoid premature and unbalanced summative judgments. Something as simple as changing the evaluative question from "Did it work?" to the more complex question "What worked for whom, in what ways and from what perspectives?" can deepen the possibility for learning and avoid an overly simplistic judgment of failure or success.

22. For a description of the tribunal, see Internews, "CTR Reports," www.internews.org/activities/kTR_reports/ICTR_reports.htm.

7. WHEN HOPE AND HISTORY RHYME

1. Candy Lightner and N. Hathaway, *Giving Sorrow Words* (New York: Warner Books, 1990).

2. *National Highway Traffic Safety Administration Report*, 1996. See http://www.alcoholalert.com/drunk-driving-statistics-2001.html.

3. Cited on the MADD website, http//www.madd.org/aboutus/1179.

4. John Dresty, "Neo-Prohibition," *The Chronicle*, May 12, 2005.

5. In the U.S. press, .10 BAC is widely understood to mean .10 blood alcohol content. Equivalencies depend on body weight, gender, food intake, length of time drinking and type of drink. To compute equivalencies for your own weight and consumption, see Minnesota State Patrol Trooper's Association, "BAC Calculator," www.mspta.com/BAC%20Calc.htm. For further detail see the following websites: Intoximeters, Inc., "Alcohol and the Human Body," www.intox.com/physiology.asp, and University of Prince Edward Island, "Blood Alcohol Levels," www.upei.ca/~stuserv/alcohol/bac1.htm.

6. David J. Hanson, "Mothers Against Drunk Driving: A Crash Course in MADD," www.alcoholfacts.org/CrashCourseOnMADD.html.

7. David J. Hanson, "Zero Tolerance," Alcohol Problems and Solutions website, www2.potsdam.edu/hansondj/ZeroTolerance.html.

8. Hanson, "Mothers," n10.

9. Columbia Accident Investigation Board 4, Final Report, 4 vols. (Washington, DC: U.S. Government Printing Office, 2003). See also http://caib.nasa.gov.

10. MSNBC, "Shuttle Report Blames NASA Culture: Investigative Panel Sees 'Systematic Flaws' That Could Set the Scene for Another Accident," August 26, 2003. www.msnbc.msn.com.

11. The Institute for Healthcare Improvement (IHI), based in Boston, is a non-profit organization dedicated to improving the quality of health care systems through education, research and demonstration projects, and through fostering collaboration among health care organizations and their leaders. IHI projects extend throughout the United States and Canada, numerous European countries, the Middle East, and elsewhere. www.ihi.org.

12. Plenary address at the 14th Annual National Forum in Quality Improvement in Health Care, Orlando, FL, December 10, 2002.

13. Stuart Kauffman, *At Home in the Universe: The Search for the Laws of Self-Organization and Complexity* (Oxford: Oxford University Press. 1996).

14. Roger Lewin, *Complexity: Life at the Edge of Chaos* (University of Chicago Press, 2000).

15. Holling and Gunderson, *Panarchy.*

16. Adapted from ibid., 75.

17. To learn about the work of Philia, see www.philia.ca.

18. E. Land, "People Should Want More from Life," *Forbes*, 1975, 48–50.

19. Adapted from Holling and Gunderson, *Panarchy.*

20. www.calmeadow.com.

21. In more technical terms, we suggest analyzing macro-micro alignments and cross-scale interactions in changing fitness landscapes.

Practice can be enhanced by forming a community of reflective practitioners devoted to macro–micro pattern recognition and reality-testing skills. Developmental evaluators can also play a role in this reflective process. Those deeply enmeshed in change can benefit from the external, more detached perspective that trained evaluators bring. We've emphasized this point over and over throughout this book. One of our goals has been to help social innovators come to see evaluation and evaluators as resources for and enablers of change rather than a hindrance. But that, we've also argued consistently, requires a different kind of evaluator, one attuned to complexity insights. So we would suggest that evaluators add to their repertoire the capacity to identify and track hope-and-history rhymes. Detecting macro-micro alignment offers a framework for bringing systems understandings into evaluation, especially making understanding of context and system dynamics central to interpreting findings.

Embedded within every evaluation is a way of thinking about the world. Entrenched in developmental evaluation are sensitivities to systems dynamics, continuous change and ongoing learning. Judging macro-micro alignment is fundamentally an evaluation problem. Interpreting a fitness landscape is fundamentally an evaluation problem. Evaluators familiar with and comfortable with these more open and emergent developmental evaluation approaches will be a better match for social innovators and the challenges they face.

This suggests that the primary challenge is to match the evaluation approach to the nature of the effort being evaluated. Where social innovators are monitoring and attending to macro-micro alignments, evaluators schooled only in traditional linear modelling and narrow goals-focused measurement will actually become barriers to rather than enhancers of innovation. To be useful and assure appropriate methods, evaluators need to adapt to the nature of the social innovation rather than imposing traditional evaluation on non-traditional innovations—beginning with being able to recognize the difference.

8. THE DOOR OPENS

1. T.S. Eliot, "Little Gidding," from *Four Quartets,* in *The Complete Poems and Plays of T.S. Eliot* (New York: Harcourt, Brace and Co., 1952), 145.

2. Adapted from Peter B. Vaill, *Learning as a Way of Being; Strategies for Survival in a World of Permanent White Water* (San Francisco: Jossey-Bass, 1996).

3. You can hear a sound clip from this interview at www.cbsg.org/ulie/soundbite.html.

4. W.B. Yeats, "Dialogue of Self and Soul," in *The Collected Works of W.B. Yeats,* Volume 1: *The Poems* (New York: Scribner), 240.

Acknowledgements

This book was inspired by the many social entrepreneurs who generously shared their experiences and reflected on our insights as we developed them. We are indebted to them all, and particularly to Cindy Blackstock, Paul Born, Jeff Brown, Bob Vokey, Vickie Cammack, Al Etmanski, Debbie Fields, Deanna Foster, Ian Gill, Mary Gordon, Jean Gornick, Richard Hill, Mary Keefe, Linda Lundström, Aaron Pereira, the late Ulysses Seal, Rusty Pritchard, Balfour Mount and Tim Brodhead. Not all the people we interviewed are mentioned by name in the book, but all of you provided inspiration and deepened our understanding of social transformation.

We give special thanks to Eric Young, a social marketer who has a brilliant capacity to create connections between ideas and between people. His work with Dupont Canada inspired the social transformation think-tank that was the source of many of the ideas in this book. He was also a vital member of that think-tank.

We are also deeply indebted to Dupont Canada, which sponsored the think-tank and hence the creation of this book. We would especially like to thank Colleen Brydon and Chris DeGrow, who participated in our think-tank meetings, and also Lori Sommers, who has continued to support our work. They were there with us as we played with outrageous ideas and had a gentle way of reining us in when we stepped too far away from reality. We are also grateful to McGill University's Faculty of Management, in particular to Rennie Nilsson and Nada Farah. They were doctoral students at the time of the think-tank, and provided excellent research support as well as fresh eyes. Simon Bird and Molly Young helped with early edits and preparation of the manuscript. Diane Marie Plante, Tara Shaughnessy and Joanne Graham worked behind the scenes to smooth our path.

Also reflected in our book is the thinking of guests we invited to our meetings. Margaret Graham, Buzz Holling, Tad Homer-Dixon, Bill Isaacs and Henry Mintzberg enriched us with their insights, creativity and critical thinking. Throughout, Tim Brodhead was a guiding light.

In the framing of developmental evaluation, special thanks goes to John Bare, Kate McKegg, Patricia Patrizi, Patricia Rogers, Bob Williams and the participants in the Developmental Evaluation seminars supported by the J.W. McConnell Family Foundation and Dupont Canada in 2005 and 2006.

We would also like to thank our editor and publisher, Anne Collins, for her insights and wise advice on improving the book. She was very patient with three academics struggling to write for an intelligent audience that wouldn't "appreciate" dry academic writing. She is a wonderful teacher. We are deeply grateful to Scott Richardson, creative director at Random House of Canada, for his innovative cover and page design.

We also want to acknowledge the extraordinary collaboration between us, which emerged as this book took shape. We came together with different backgrounds, expertise and experiences, but with a shared commitment to the ideals and vision expressed in these pages. We had many exciting discussions where we experienced hours of flow. We each got stuck at times, but never, thankfully, all of us at the same time, and so we were able to pull each other along the unfolding path. We divided the labour of writing specific chapters, but ultimately all the chapters became shared endeavours, a product of our times together in Montreal, Toronto, Madison, Wisconsin, and the mountains of Colorado, as well as ongoing email communications. Although we have finished writing the book, our work together will continue as we look for deeper insights into and applications of complexity perspectives in support of social innovators.

Last but certainly not least, we would also like to thank our spouses, Fred Bird, Bryan Hayday and Jeanne Campbell, for their loving support and their confidence that we would eventually get to maybe!

—

We dedicate this book to our children—Rebecca, Bruce, Katie, Clara, Jane, Stephanie, Gillian, Matthew, Catherine, Sarah, Brandon, Charmagne and Quinn—who will know whether we got there or not.

Index

Notes: Page numbers in italic indicate a figure or table. The letter *n* indicates a note; for example "231*n*3" refers to note 3 on page 231.

as partners in fighting poverty, 149–50
demand accountability, 179–80
Grameen Bank
 begins, 55, 58–59, 61, 84
 overcomes rigidity trap, 68
 relies on shared information and
  relationships, 134–35
 success, 55, 60, 81, 211–12

Hammond, Ray, 32–34
health care
 palliative, 16–20, 114–16, 225
 shift to patient-centred care, 199–202
Heaney, Seamus, 188–89
HIV/AIDS
 Brazil's successful campaign to slow,
  4–6, 10, 135–40
 infection rates, 4–5
 North American movement, 96–99
Holling, C.S. "Buzz," 65–67, 69, 72, 99,
  206
Hope Community, Minneapolis, 171,
  175, 237n15
Hurricane Katrina, 42–43
Hutu people, 162–63

Ignatieff, Michael, 209
improvisation, 153–54, 235–36n16–17
individuals
 as resources, 5, 7, 43, 135–38, 200
 collectively generate energy and
  momentum toward change,
  130–31, 133, 155
 relationships create social
  innovation, 4, 6–7, 10, 16, 19
 resilience, 66
information
 importance of target, 156–57
 must resonate with local experience,
  133
 shared
  creates flow, 133–35

enables Grameen Bank, 134–35
 enables self-organization, 143–44
 importance of, 158, 236n19
inner cities
 children's safety area, 172–75
 gang violence reduction, 30–35,
  44–45
 importance of positive role models,
  16–19
 women's shelter, 170–71
Institute for Healthcare Improvement,
  200, 241n11
Iraq, U.S. invasion of, 23, 86

Jacobs, Jane, 139, 142–44

Kauffman, Stuart, 202
Keefe, Mary, 171–75
Keller, Evelyn, 132
Kiishik Fund, 15
Kingwell, Mark, 209
Kitchener-Waterloo, Ontario, 145–53,
  227–28
Krugman, Paul, 142–44
Kübler-Ross, Elizabeth, 116
Kuntz, Ted, 75

Land, Edwin, 130, 209–10
language as barrier, 107–8
leaders
 as partners with community, 84, 106,
  152
 as those with ability to manage
  patterns, 142
 risk of hubris, 197
 social innovators as, but not by
  standard model, 20, 37–38,
  132–33, 139, 142
learning disorders, 11
liberation theology, 5, 136
Lightner, Candy
 begins MADD, 191–92, 203

Permissions

Deming, Alison Hawthorne, "Urban Law" from *Genius Loci*. Used by permission of the author.

Cohen, Leonard and Sharon Robinson, "Everybody Knows" from the album Cohen Live. Copyright © 1988. Stranger Music Inc. (BMI).

Oliver, Mary, "Wild Geese" from *Dream Work*. Copyright © 1986 by Mary Oliver. Published by Atlantic Monthly Press.

Heaney, Seamus, "Doubletake" from *The Cure at Troy*. Used by permission of Faber and Faber Ltd.

Rich, Adrienne, "Prospective Immigrants Please Note". Copyright © 2002, 1967, 1963 by Adrienne Rich, from *The Fact of a Doorframe: Selected Poems 1950–2001* by Adrienne Rich. Used by permission of the author and W.W. Norton & Company, Inc.